Color Moves
Transfer Paints on Fabric

Color Moves

Transfer Paints on Fabric

LINDA KEMSHALL

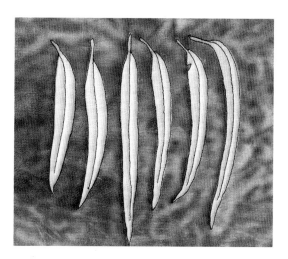

& COMPANY

WOODINVILLE, WASHINGTON

CREDITS

President / Nancy J. Martin
CEO/Publisher / Daniel J. Martin
Associate Publisher / Jane Hamada
Editorial Director / Mary V. Green
Editorial Project Manager / Tina Cook
Technical Editor / Jane Townswick
Copy Editor / Ellen Balstad
Design and Production Manager / Stan Green
Illustrator / Laurel Strand
Photographer / Brent Kane
Cover and Interior Designer / Stan Green

That Patchwork Place is an imprint of
Martingale & Company.

Color Moves: Transfer Paints on Fabric
© 2001 by Linda Kemshall

Martingale & Company
20205 144th Avenue NE
Woodinville, WA 98072-8478 USA
www.martingale-pub.com

Printed in China
06 05 04 03 02 01   8 7 6 5 4 3 2 1

Mission Statement
We are dedicated to providing quality products
and service by working together to inspire
creativity and to enrich the lives we touch.

Library of Congress Cataloging-in-Publication Data

Kemshall, Linda.
    Color moves : transfer paints on fabric / Linda Kemshall.
        p. cm.
    ISBN 1-56477-341-8
    1. Transfer-printing. 2. Textile printing. I. Title.

TT852.7 .K46 2001
746.6—dc21   00-050006

DEDICATION

This book is dedicated to my family by way of an apology
for all the dinners not cooked, the beds not made, the shirts not ironed,
and the rooms not dusted. Life is too short to be remembered
only for keeping a tidy house!

Contents

Introduction

Including photographs and images in quilts and fabric projects has become very popular recently. Most of these images are transferred to fabric with the use of computer-image transfer techniques, or by photocopying onto special heat-sensitive paper and then ironing the images to the fabric. Other methods involve transferring an image from a photocopy with an acrylic adhesive. Many of these processes leave a shiny, plastic residue layer, which traps the picture and protects the inks so that the fabrics can be washed. Unfortunately, this shiny layer alters the hand of the fabric, making it stiff and difficult to stitch. Surprisingly, there are other ways to add color and images that are easy to do, don't add a plastic layer to your fabric, require only simple tools and equipment, result in very individual work, and yet seem little exploited by textile artists. These techniques are the foundation for *Color Moves*.

The disperse dyes described in this book (all transfer products include these dyes as one of their ingredients) are used extensively in the industrial fabric-printing industry to add color and pattern to synthetic fabrics. They are, however, almost overlooked by quiltmakers and embroiderers as a potentially valuable part of their creative vocabulary. Like most worthwhile things, a little patience is needed. Any efforts you make to experiment and develop ideas will be rewarded. You can learn the basic techniques for transfer printing easily by following the instructions that come with the paints and dyes, but technique is only part of the picture. Using methods creatively involves consideration and imagination. I hope that the suggestions and guidelines in this book will inspire you to try these image-transfer products and processes, especially if they are new to you. If you have already tried them but with limited success, I encourage you to reconsider the part they might play in enriching your own creativity. Often the most exciting effects come from a combination or layering of techniques, rather than a single application. I find that redeeming a so-called "failure" by working with it can often produce interesting and unexpected results.

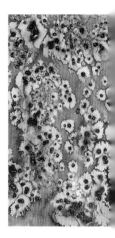

When I began to write this book, I really thought I knew all I needed to know to put it together. However, I quickly found myself heeding the advice that I continually give my students—take nothing for granted; experiment; sample; question; keep records of outcomes, both good and bad, and if you have even half an idea that something might work, then just do it. I made new discoveries every time I tried out an idea, and then that idea made me think of the next thing to try. I thoroughly enjoyed the process of experimentation and the luxury of concentrating on one subject at a time. My teaching involves all aspects of design, patchwork, quilting, appliqué, paper-making, and mixed media. It is all too easy, when you are interested in so many things, to skim the surface of a subject without ever having the time to explore its potential fully. The challenge of writing a book and the motivation that an impending deadline affords gave me the inspiration to delve deeper. I feel that for

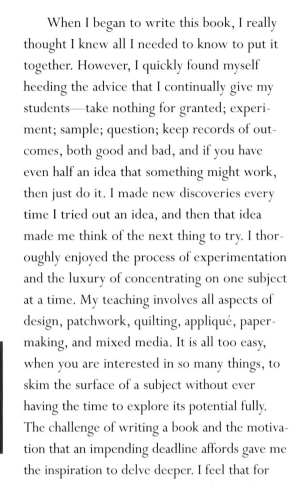

once I have been able to get the best from these methods, because the more time you invest, the greater the rewards. Read my book and benefit from what I have learned, and then take it further and make your own discoveries. With an open mind and enough curiosity to ask yourself, What if? you will be liberated from relying on somebody else's experiences, and will find that all things are possible.

Linda Kemshall

SECTION 1

Transfer-Printing Supplies and Instructions

A range of products was used to create the samples and projects in this book. The one thing that all of the projects have in common is the use of transfer printing in some form or other. Transfer printing involves applying color to paper, allowing the paper to dry, and then transferring and fixing the color to fabric with heat. In commercial practice, a heat press is used, but I like to keep everything simple and accessible to anyone by using a domestic iron and only the most basic and available equipment possible.

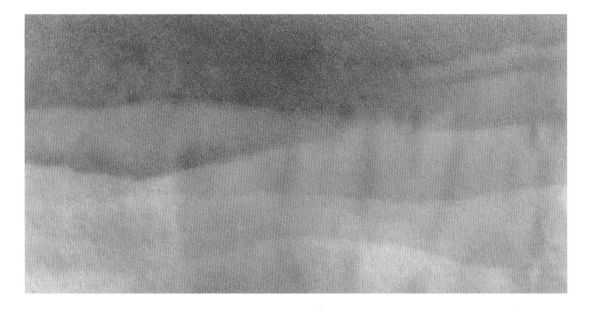

The pigments found in the transfer dyes, inks, and paints used in the projects for this book were designed for use on synthetic fabrics and blends with a minimum of 60 percent synthetic content. Some color transfers to cotton, but it is neither light- nor colorfast on a natural fiber. For years now, quiltmakers have done their very best to work only with pure and natural fibers, and now I am suggesting that you actually seek out those synthetics you have tried to avoid for so long! Fabrics have come a long way in recent years and there are some gorgeous polyesters and poly/cotton blends available. Take a look at the samples in this book and decide if you can be lured away from cotton long enough to experiment with the techniques described in the next few pages. I hope you can.

Seek out those synthetics you have tried to avoid for so long!

Transfer paints, dyes, pens, and crayons all produce brilliant colors on pure polyester and very satisfactory, vibrant results on mixed fibers. Most importantly, they do not alter the hand of the fabric they are applied to, as many fabric paints can. When you are intending to hand quilt a piece, it is so unpleasant to have to stitch through a fabric stiffened with paint. Although the prints have to be made on synthetics or blends, you can combine them with cotton or silk in a patchwork project. The colors I work with in this book are found in a variety of guises. The following supplies should be readily available wherever you live, and I have suggested a few suppliers in "Resources" on page 93 who offer mail-order services. Increasingly, supplies are also available via the Internet, so I have also included Web site addresses in "Resources" whenever possible. All the products that I suggest are sold as nontoxic. The resulting prints are washable and can be dry-cleaned.

Transfer Paints

Transfer paints are sold in liquid form and come in small plastic or glass containers. They are available in a limited range of colors, but they can be mixed together and are thick enough to use in printing techniques.

Transfer Inks

Transfer inks are also sold in liquid form and are a little thinner than transfer paints; they have the consistency of drawing inks. The pigment in the inks can settle, so it is a good idea to stir or shake transfer inks before using them. The inks are interchangeable with the transfer paints for many of the techniques in this book. If the inks' fluidity becomes a disadvantage, you can thicken them by adding a stock solution made from a product recommended by the ink manufacturer. Don't be tempted to use a thickener that you have on hand. Make sure you use the kind recommended by the manufacturer. Some thickeners, even though they may be effective in thickening the ink, can inhibit the transfer of color when you print.

A stock paste is a type of thickener that you can mix by hand or with a blender. Follow the manufacturer's guidelines for quantities. The dye and ink manufacturers assure me that the thickeners I use are made of a type of gum, which is a common food additive and can be mixed in a kitchen blender. However, I prefer to be safe with paints and dyes, and use a blender that I specifically bought for craft projects. Once the inks are thicker, they can be used for things like monoprinting and stamping. In my experience, the range of colors of transfer inks is wider than that of transfer paints.

Disperse Powder Dyes

Disperse powder dyes are a specially designed range of concentrated powder dyes for coloring polyester and other synthetic fabrics with transfer methods. They are the pigments found in all the other transfer products and are available in large or small quantities for mixing as needed. Powder dyes are made viable by adding them to tepid water and following the manufacturers' guidelines. Once mixed they will keep for years, as long as a thickening substance has not been added. As in transfer inks, the pigments are held in suspension in water and can settle to the bottom of the storage container. Make sure you stir or shake the storage container before using powder dyes, or you may get a disappointingly pale print. Mixing your own dyes is usually more economical than buying them premixed, so this method is recommended for group work and large-scale pieces. Disperse powder dyes offer the advantage of allowing you to control the strength of color. They can also be used to dye a pale fabric with a new base color before any transfer printing. See "Section 2: Beyond the Basics" on page 24 for details.

Transfer Crayons

Transfer crayons are designed for use with synthetics and synthetic blends. Images drawn with transfer crayons are transferred indirectly to the fabric from a paper print. This process differs from fabric crayons, which you use to draw directly on fabric. Transfer crayons are pigments held in a solid, waxy substance that can be packaged to look and be used just like children's crayon. I think that the colors can be crude, although I once saw some French transfer crayons whose colors were very subtle. It may take a little more thought, but pleasing results can be achieved with them by *overprinting*, or transfer printing over another image already printed on the fabric. Using more than one color in a print or using a background fabric that has already been colored in an interesting way are other options. The main advantages of the crayons are their immediacy—no drying time needed—and the ease and speed with which rubbings can be made with them from a huge variety of relief or textured surfaces. Transfer crayons are an ideal fabric-coloring medium for beginners, one that children can use safely with a minimal amount of mess involved. Even very young children can draw directly on a piece of paper from which a print will be made, though they will need adult help with the printing process. In this way, their original artwork can be preserved for years to come. Crayons can also be combined with transfer inks in a single design for more complex and sophisticated effects. See "Rubbings and Resists" on page 49 for more information.

Transfer Pens

Transfer pens are not readily available everywhere, but if you find some, they are useful for adding fine details and for graphic, linear work.

Testing the Products

Try out samples of your chosen products before launching into a major project, as it is likely that the colors of the paints or dyes will not print onto fabric exactly as they appear on paper. Sometimes the difference is very surprising. The only sure way of predicting your results is to test your transfer medium on the same fabric you will be working with in your project. The colors will appear rather dull and unexciting on paper, but be reassured that they will show their true brilliance when heat is applied. The photo below shows one range of transfer paints as they look on paper and the resulting prints on a white poly/cotton blend. These colors were used straight from the jars, without any mixing or addition of water. On the left, you can see that the paint was applied as a flat color, which prints as a solid area. On the right, the paint was roughly applied to the paper with the intention of leaving brush marks in the color. Notice how the texture marks are more apparent in the second print, and perhaps even more obvious, though more pale, in the third.

The only sure way of predicting your results is to test.

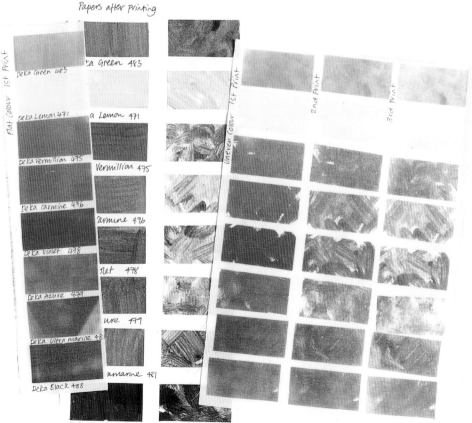

Papers after printing

Flat Colour 1st Print

Deka Green 483 — a Green 483

Deka Lemon 471 — a Lemon 471

Deka Vermillian 475 — Vermillian 475

Deka Carmine 476 — armine 476

Deka Violet 478 — et 478

Deka Azure 479 — ure 479

Deka Ultra marine 48 — amarine 481

Deka Black 488

Deka Black 488

Uneven Colour 1st Print

2nd Print

3rd Print

Use a color chart to evaluate the effects of the dyes and transfer medium you plan to use.

These unmixed colors aren't very interesting, but "Section 2: Beyond the Basics" shows how they can be made more appealing with careful handling. What makes all these products different from other fabric-coloring media is that in nearly all cases they are applied to paper first. The paper is allowed to dry, and the color is then transferred to fabric with a hot iron. Most of the painted papers retain enough color to enable them to be used several times, even though each print becomes successively weaker as the color is exhausted. As explained earlier, the best results are achieved on polyester, but nylon, Tricel (cellulose triacetate), and acrylic also work well. If in doubt, it is always worth experimenting on a scrap of fabric to determine its potential. For example, I have created some wonderful prints on a stretch fabric normally used to make leotards.

Working Safely

All of the products used in this book are considered nontoxic by their manufacturers, but it makes good sense to observe a few basic rules when working with dye materials. Also note that manufacturers provide safety guidelines, so be sure to read them before starting any project. Mixing your own pigments from powders is the point at which I feel a problem is most likely to occur. The fine powders can be inhaled if they are allowed to float around in the air, so work away from drafty areas and wear a mask. Cover your work surfaces with damp newspapers so that accidental powder spills will stick and give you time to clean up safely. Whenever possible, prevent dye materials from touching your skin. Protect your hands with rubber gloves. However, if you should happen to get these materials on your skin, wash immediately with copious amounts of water. When discharge printing (see page 44), avoid any contact between your skin and the bleach products.

Not all of us have the luxury of a separate work area that can be dedicated to our art and craft projects. However, it is really important to keep all dye materials away from food-and-drink preparation areas, and never to use containers or utensils that are normally used for cooking. In fact, any equipment used for dyeing should be used only for dyeing. If you make up more dye than you can use in a single printing session, keep it until the next time you need it, but make sure you label the container clearly and store it in a safe place away from children. Manufacturers tell me that as long as thickener has not been added to a dye solution it will have a shelf life of several years. Transfer paints and inks do not need to be mixed and are nontoxic, so you might find these more convenient for children to work with, especially in a busy classroom.

There is a certain amount of odor released when painted papers are ironed onto fabric, but this should not present any problems under normal circumstances. Always work in a room with adequate ventilation, especially if several people are working together, which will multiply the effects. At the end of a session, any paints or dyes that remain in a mixing palette should be sponged quickly onto some sheets of paper. Disposing of the leftovers this way eliminates waste, and you will also create some interesting images to transfer.

Choosing Fabrics

All of the techniques in this book are intended for use with either pure synthetics, like polyester, or blended fibers that have a synthetic content of 60 percent or higher.

Before printing, your fabrics should be thoroughly washed, dried, and ironed, unless they are specifically sold as "ready for dyeing and painting." Washing fabrics removes sizing, which is applied during the manufacturing process to make the fabrics look and handle better on the bolt. If the sizing is not washed away before you begin your project, the surface of the fabric will be less receptive to color, the bond between the dyes and fibers may be weaker, and some color may be lost when the item is washed.

Dyes produce a transparent layer of color, which is most apparent on a white or pale background fabric. You can make additional prints on top of the first, like a painter adding washes of color to build a rich and complex image. Remember that normal rules of color theory apply. If, for instance, a yellow print is ironed over a blue print or fabric, a greenish print will be the result. It is always easiest to start pale and add darker elements to a design, because the transparent color of these dyes can modify but not completely obscure previous layers.

Pure polyester works beautifully, but so do many other synthetics. I encourage you to try as many different types of synthetic fabrics as possible. Search through leftover garment-making fabrics and your scrap bag for samples before committing to large purchases. Buy a large quantity of fabric only when you are

A range of synthetic and poly-cotton blend fabrics with at least 60 percent synthetic content

TIP Small fabric scraps are fine as trial pieces. Glue them into a notebook with brief annotations on the transfer product and methods you used. This notebook will be a great resource for future reference.

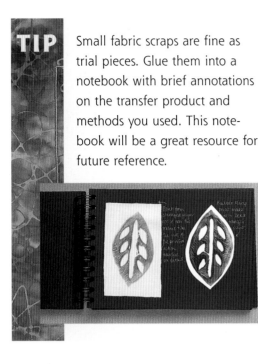

makes a suitable base for techniques such as embroidery and appliqué. It is very absorbent, however, and takes much of the available color from the paper. Second prints are rarely worth the effort because of this.

Please note that the color is transferred by ironing, so it is vital to choose fabrics that can withstand the heat needed to sublimate the dye. I always place parchment paper over my materials when I do my printing; this helps the iron glide gently without disturbing the print paper below. It also protects the edges of the fabric not covered by the painted paper and prevents possible scorching.

happy with your results. Ask friends and relatives to contribute items such as old sheer curtains and linings.

Experiment with a range of fabric weights too. Sheer voiles will print successfully, producing delicate, transparent color that is ideal for layering and stitching. Some color passes through delicate fabric, so place a second layer of fabric below the first and make two prints simultaneously.

Lacy fabrics not only accept color but also act as a mask, allowing some color to pass through the holes onto a layer of fabric below—two for the price of one! Synthetic velvets are lustrous and gorgeous when colored, but care has to be taken to flatten the pile as little as possible when ironing.

Transfer printing is also an ideal technique for delicate fabrics which drape easily and which do not respond well to less sensitive applications of color. Nonwoven interfacing also accepts color beautifully and

Transfer printing on delicate fabrics

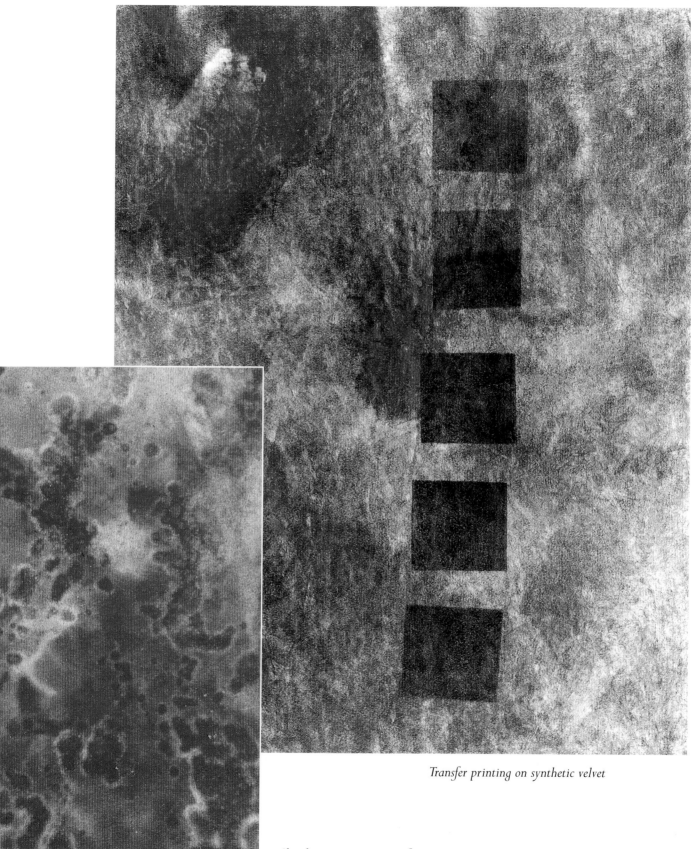

Transfer printing on synthetic velvet

Absorbent nonwoven interfacing

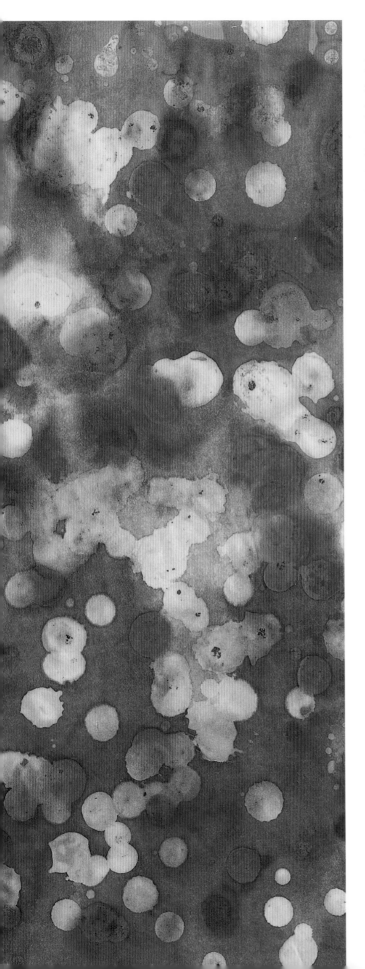

Selecting Paper

In order to take the color from transfer paints, inks, or crayons, smooth, strong, nonporous paper is required. Wet color also needs to be allowed to dry thoroughly. If you are feeling impatient, it is possible to speed up the drying time by using a hair dryer. However, if the paper wrinkles, the print may be adversely affected, so natural drying is preferable. After it is painted and dry, the paper can be trimmed or cut to shape as necessary, and printed.

Use as high a temperature on your iron as the fabric will tolerate. It is important not to choose paper that is too thick, because this hinders the passage of heat to the fabric. Photocopy paper is ideal; it is not too absorbent, which would be a wasteful and extravagant use of pigment, and it is not too thick to suppress the heat-transfer process. It also works well for crayon rubbings, where it is essential to have a sensitive yet strong paper that is not too thick.

Use photocopy paper for crayon rubbings.

TIP If you like using a computer to help with drawing and design, you will find it offers easy ways to reverse shapes and do other techniques such as tiling. Print out the results on plain paper, and then follow the suggestions for applying color and printing.

Layout paper used by graphic artists is also worth considering because it is semitranspar-ent, which gives it an advantage over opaque photocopy paper when you are working with a design that you need to reverse before print-ing, such as text. The letters or shapes can be traced or drawn on one side and then the layout paper flipped over to show the reversed design. The paint is applied to this reverse side and will read properly when printed.

Basic Transfer Printing

STARTING A JOURNAL

It's a good idea to record details about all the various products you try as you begin to do transfer printing. It is amazing how deceptive some paints can be, changing as they are placed

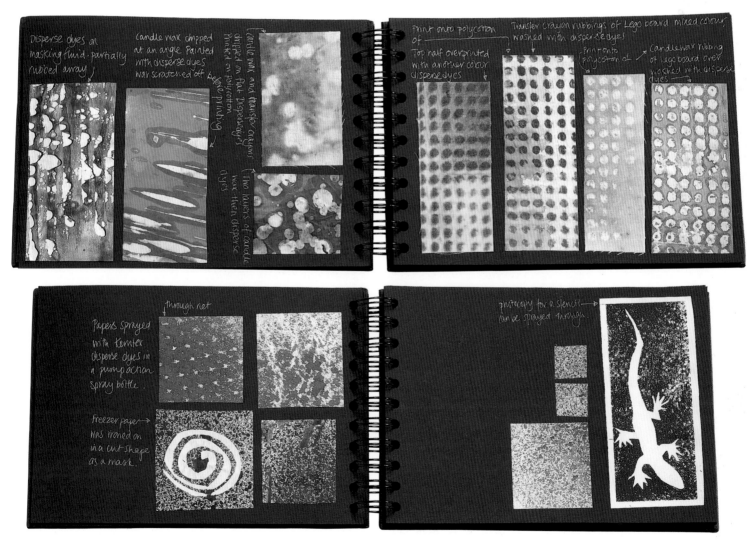

Keep notes and samples in a journal of all the various transfer-printing techniques you try.

on the paper and printing in unexpected ways. Make notes on the reverse of your painted papers as you work, and add pertinent comments in your notebook. Keep samples of the papers and fabric so you can avoid future mistakes and confidently repeat your good results whenever you wish.

Also take notes about the various transfer-printing processes you try, and add comments about different techniques, papers, and fabrics. Keeping an ongoing journal is a great way to make sure that everything you learn and experience is always at your fingertips for future projects, and it can inspire new ideas and techniques as well.

DIRECTIONS

For your first transfer-printing experience, pick a project that is straightforward and simple. Use paints or inks without diluting or mixing them. If you have powder dyes, make up solutions according to the manufacturer's guidelines. Two colors will be fine to get started. It isn't necessary to have an artist's palette for mixing colors (you can mix the colors directly on the paper), but try not to dirty the paint containers by using the same brush in more than one color. Yellow is especially vulnerable to contamination, and dirties to green quickly. To begin, paint either a whole sheet of paper or a simple shape, like a square drawn with pencil. Use quick, broad brush strokes, and aim for a fairly smooth and generous layer of color.

Once you have painted your design, leave the paper on a flat surface to dry. It is important that the paper is completely dry before printing.

Use quick, broad brush strokes when painting paper.

Let paper dry completely on a flat surface.

TIP If you have opted to paint a shape, you can create a clean image by trimming away any unwanted background paper, especially if there are little splashes and drips where there shouldn't be. A well-defined cut shape is also easier to align when printing repeats to make a pattern.

Brush strokes create interesting textures in the finished project.

While the paint is drying, you can prepare your printing area. I have found that a hard surface produces the best results. A wooden table or laminated worktop is ideal. If you choose to work on a fairly small project, an old wooden breadboard would also make a good choice for a work surface.

Since it is very likely that some color will pass through the fabric when you are ironing, protect your work surface from stains and heat by covering it with a couple of sheets of newspaper. Make sure you put a sheet of clean white paper on top of the newspaper, because it is also very easy to transfer newspaper text in reverse. Place the piece of fabric to be colored on top of the printing area and the paper with your design facedown on top of it. Put a sheet of parchment paper over the whole area so that any fabric not covered by the prepared paper is protected. Next, with your iron temperature set as high as the fabric will allow and the steam turned off, press the iron firmly while gently and slowly gliding it from side to side all over the transfer. Transferring the design can take a couple of minutes for small prints, but the time must be increased for larger designs to ensure that all areas get sufficient heat. Bear in mind that the temperature may not be constant across the base of the entire iron. It is therefore important to keep the iron moving so that all areas of the design transfer consistently.

Cover fabric and prepared transfer design (facedown) with parchment paper to protect the fabric.

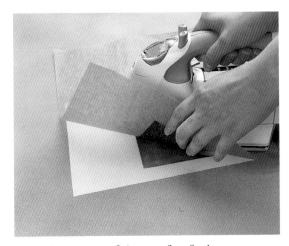

Check the progress of the transfer of color.

 Keep the iron moving, or the steam holes on the soleplate of your iron will appear on your fabric!

Corners and edges are particularly easy to miss, so pay attention when you get to these areas. While pressing carefully, lift a corner of the paper to check the progress of the transfer of color, but take care not to move the rest of the paper or the image will be blurred.

Stop ironing when you are satisfied with the quality and strength of your print. There will usually be enough dye remaining on the paper to repeat the printing process several times, with each print becoming paler as the color is used up.

TIP

I often prefer the third or fourth print from a single paper because the textures created when applying the color become increasingly evident as some of the dye is removed. The resulting transfers on synthetics will be very fast and will withstand a hot wash, if required. The first time they are washed there might be a slight loss of excess color. Remember, most disappointing prints result from insufficient heat or lack of time allowed for the dyes to sublimate!

Paper with design has enough dye remaining to repeat the printing process.

SECTION 2

Beyond the Basics

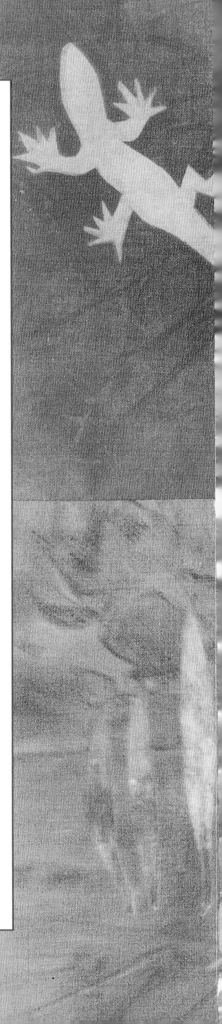

*A*fter you've learned the basics of transfer printing, it's time to move on and explore the exciting ways you can work with color, fabric, and paper to produce unique effects.

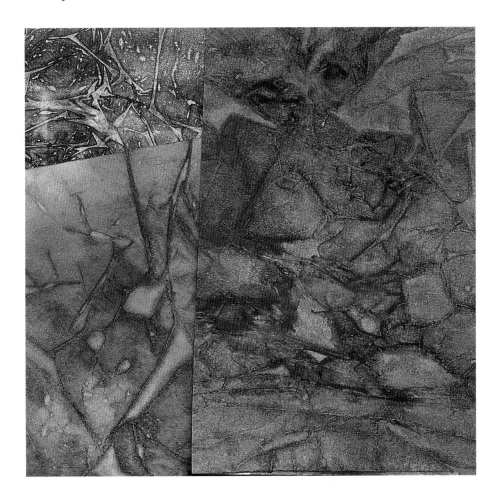

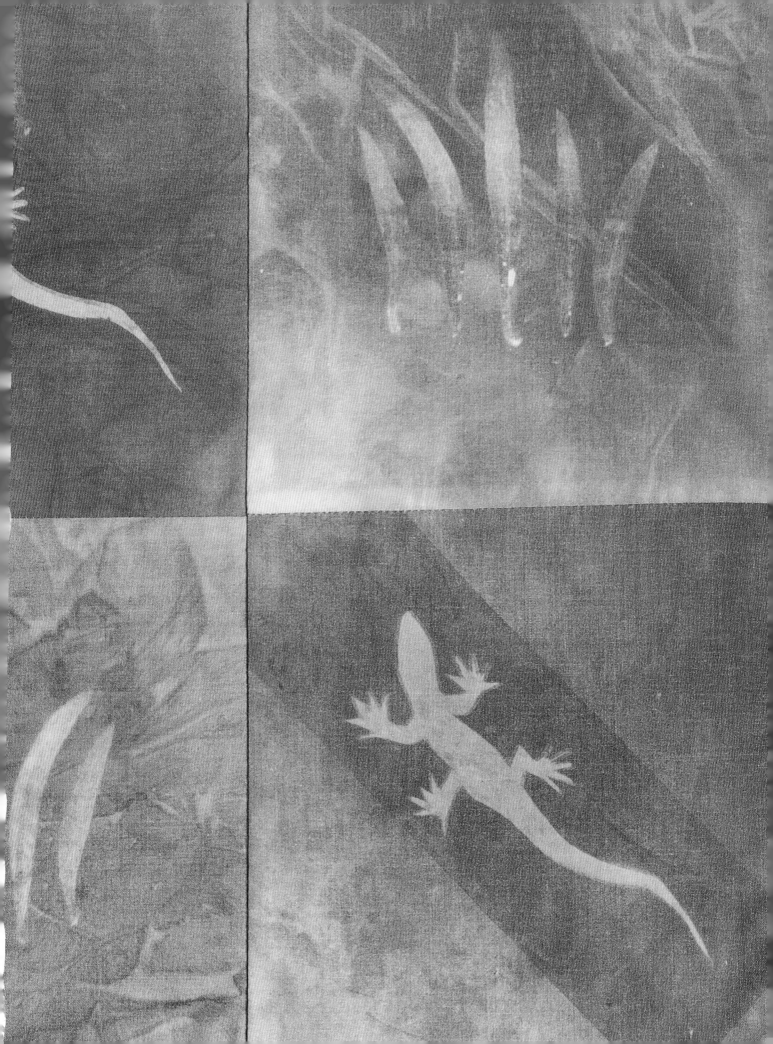

Applying Color to Fabrics

Read through the following techniques and try them to see which ones are your favorites.

SCRUNCH PRINTING

One simple variation on the basic color-transfer method is to crumple the fabric and iron a sheet of paper with transfer color over the folds and creases. The fabric can be opened, rescrunched, and reprinted as many times as needed to create interesting colors and shapes.

HOT-WATER DYEING

You can color synthetic fabrics with disperse dyes and a conventional hot-water dyeing process. This process is a useful way of preparing a base color other than white.

Although polyester fabrics are made in a wide range of commercially dyed, solid-color pastel shades ideal for transfer-printinmg

Scrunch-printed fabric

Create a base color other than white with the hot-water dyeing process. The sample shown here has a yellow base color.

projects, you may not find a store near you that carries a good selection. If you choose to dye your own fabric for this or another reason, you can follow this simple recipe.

The disperse dyes that I use (Kemtex-brand transprint dyes; see "Resources" on page 93) require that you sprinkle a small quantity of the appropriate dye color into a large volume of tepid water in a heatproof pot. I add the prewashed, damp polyester fabric and heat it up slowly over 30 minutes to the simmering point. Then I allow it to continue simmering for another 20 minutes. It is important to keep the fabric submerged and to stir frequently for even dyeing. I allow the fabric to cool, and

then rinse it under running water to wash any unfixed color away. The fabric is then left to dry. After it is ironed, it will be ready for use. Darker colors can be achieved by increasing dye quantities, but dark fabric is less successful as a printing ground because the print doesn't show clearly against a dark color. Remember that color contrast has to be present in order to achieve well-defined shapes on a printing background.

SPACE DYEING

For a really gorgeous effect, I prefer to treat fabrics with space dyeing, which creates lovely painterly effects and provides a compatible background for subsequent print applications. Use the hot-water dyeing technique described in the previous section, but increase the amount of fabric or decrease the amount of water, so that the fabric is never completely submerged. This produces uneven coloring results. It is important to keep an eye on the

Space-dyed velvet

pot when you reduce the amount of liquid, because the fabric can burn if the pot boils dry.

An alternative method can also produce beautiful effects, but without the need for simmering. For this, you will need a container suitable for your fabric. A plastic cat-litter tray is perfect and inexpensive, but you can also use an old container such as a plastic ice-cream tub if you want to be really thrifty. Place damp, crumpled polyester fabric into the tray or tub, and pour or spoon some dye solution onto it. Judge the quantity by eye, keeping in mind that the color will creep along the folds of the damp cloth and gradually cover the white areas as it spreads. Don't be over generous with the dye; you don't want pools of color to form in the bottom of the container. The fabric must remain in the tray until it is completely dry, so be patient; this may take several days if the weather is cool or damp, especially if you are using a heavy fabric that absorbs more liquid. In the summer you can leave the tray or tub outside in the sun to speed up the drying process. The crumpling of the fabric will help interesting patterns to form. Where the fabric touches the bottom of the container, shapes in the dye color are created.

Once your fabric is dry, you'll be able to see the gorgeous colors. Fix the colors by ironing the fabric without any steam at the highest temperature the fabric will stand. It helps if you iron both sides of the fabric. The space-dyeing method is not as reliably colorfast as transferring color from paper, because more dye is involved; the dye is held all through the fibers rather than only on the surface. It is therefore more difficult to achieve the close contact between the fabric and the base of the

Space-dyed fabrics

iron which is needed to fix the color permanently. This is particularly true of a velvet pile, but it is worth the effort to obtain such rich results.

A heat press is ideal for fixing color. However, since few of us have access to such a tool, persevere with your own iron and don't rush this part of the process in your enthusiasm to use the lovely fabric you have created. After ironing, wash the fabric with a gentle detergent to remove excess dye; the color that remains is permanent. The example shown below, though beautiful, would only work as background fabric if the design to be transfer-printed were in black, because the background fabric colors are so intense. For paler results, you can simply reduce the amount of dye used.

This dark fabric requires a black transfer-printing design; any other color would not show.

Applying Color to Paper

Once you have mastered the basic technique of painting paper and transferring color to fabric with heat, the real fun of experimentation can begin.

USING A PAINTBRUSH

To create printed areas of flat, solid color, paint the paper as evenly and smoothly as possible with transfer paints. Use a broad paintbrush and work quickly, or dark lines might show where the edges of the paint begin to dry before a second stroke overlaps it. Paint right up to the edges of the paper to create the largest usable area for transferring color. Try to avoid leaving brush marks if you can, because this technique is very sensitive and any marks in the paint will print as lines. Even fine lines such as those made by the bristles of the brush will be visible.

Using a paintbrush to apply color to paper is a sensitive technique; any brush marks in paint will print lines.

When the painted image is transferred to fabric, the fabric will have plain, solid areas of color or a mixture of colors you choose. These solid colors are a good fabric background choice for overprinting geometric shapes. Color can be applied using the dyeing techniques described previously or with one of the special-effect techniques described in the next few pages. Remember that for a second print to show clearly, you need to create contrast, either by using different colors or different values of color—dark to light. Dark colors, such as violet, navy blue, and deep red, stand out clearly on most light- to medium-value background fabrics.

In addition to solid color, it is also possible with a paintbrush to create the effect of texture on fabric. Texture is usually thought to describe the qualities of a surface as determined by touch: the fingertips detect relief or roughness in the surface. But a smooth surface can be given visual texture or the appearance of relief or roughness. With the transfer process, you can create visual texture by including such things as lines, splatters, or small-scale pattern details on the paper. Uneven color often suggests depth and perspective too. Think about the space-dyed fabrics described earlier and how they are so much more interesting than a solid color.

TIP A dry, coarse hog-bristle brush will make scratchy, distinct lines. I sometimes like to allow the colors to intermingle on the page rather than premixing them on a palette. There is a certain amount of unpredictability about this method but lots of opportunity for happy accidents and serendipity.

Use a stencil brush to create swirls of color on paper.

Instead of aiming for flat, even color, try for the exact opposite. Leave the marks of the brush in the paint. Put the paint onto the paper as roughly as you can. The more marks or details you leave in the paint the better, because this creates more visual interest. Paints or dyes with added thickener are best suited to this technique. Dyes without thickeners are more fluid, which allows them to flow easily and spread over the paper with more even coverage. Try a variety of brushes, since this also will influence the sort of marks that you can make. For example, soft and generous watercolor brushes leave an elegant, tapering, feather-like shape. A big, chunky stenciling brush used vertically on the paper produces completely different results from a soft, flat artist's brush.

Many different textures are possible with the use of a paintbrush.

WORKING WITH COLOR COMPLEMENTS

You can create the most beautiful and subtle variations of color by working with pairs of complementary colors. Complementary colors lie opposite each other on a color wheel—blue and orange, red and green, violet and yellow. Surprisingly, pleasing neutrals result from mixing these opposite pairs. Grays and browns created this way will have vitality and warmth. Mixed opposites retain the character of their original components. Watercolor artists have long known that it is best to avoid black when depicting the natural world. It is much more effective to add deep violet shadows to a sunny golden landscape than to include dead-looking black areas. If your paints and dyes seem too bright to use straight from the jar, try adding a hint of the complement color, which will subdue the intensity of the color. It may sound surprising to suggest adding a touch of violet to yellow, for example, but the result is a gentle color. A little more violet produces an ochre yellow, whereas adding black to yellow creates a very dirty green. Take some time to play with color! The more you experiment, the more control you will have over the outcomes. For example, you will find that you can create lovely olive greens by adding a hint of red to green, and terra-cotta is simply orange that has been subdued by adding blue.

Obviously, the quality of the color you start with will influence the results of your color mixing. Is your blue a turquoise or a navy? Is your red a tomatoey scarlet or a cool crimson? The most saturated oranges need warm scarlet, and the most saturated purples need cool alizarin crimson. Clear violet is the most difficult color to achieve, which explains

TIP Some people are timid about mixing colors. If this sounds like you, find a book on color theory that is aimed at the amateur artist. The same color rules apply to paints as well as to dyes. Remember that any unpainted paper will appear as white in your finished print (unless your base fabric is already colored or printed).

why it is the most expensive pigment in the artists' palette and why flower painters buy it ready-mixed. In theory, you should be able to create all the colors you might possibly want from the three primary colors—red, blue, and yellow. In reality, you will actually require two of each of those basic colors to have any kind of control over the results of your color mixing. If the product you are buying features a choice (and not all of them do), choose a golden yellow and a lemon, a scarlet and a crimson, and a turquoise and an ultramarine. By combining these six colors and changing the proportions of the mixes slightly, you can create the widest and most subtle range of colors imaginable.

SPECIAL EFFECTS
WITH PLASTIC WRAP

An exciting way of introducing visual texture to a print is to apply color to the paper and then, while the paint or ink is still wet, place a sheet of plastic wrap such as Saran Wrap onto the surface. Crease the plastic with your fingers, and watch how the color is held in the folds. Leave the paper to dry completely before peeling away the plastic wrap. Interesting, hard-edged shapes will remain, ready to be transferred to your fabric. The marks will have a very organic appearance, and can be made to resemble leaf veins or tree branches. Choose your colors with care and you will be able to suggest striations in rock or marble, or facets in crystals.

The plastic-wrap technique works with either dye or paint, but because of the difference in the thickness of the two products, the effects you get will not be quite the same. If you have both paints and dyes, try sampling each. Experiment with a range of papers, too, because this will also affect your results. A slightly shiny paper seems to be a good choice for this technique.

A crumpled plastic bag is another material you might try to use to create a pattern in your wet color. Plastic bubble wrap, bubble side down to the paint, also makes a good contact print. Place a magazine on top to improve the contact between plastic and paper, and leave it undisturbed until the paint or dye is completely dry.

Interesting patterns made with plastic wrap and photocopy paper

Use shiny paper for the plastic-wrap technique to create lines with hard edges.

SPECIAL EFFECTS WITH SALT

If you have tried the salt technique in silk painting, you know just how it works. On paper, though, the technique takes a little longer. To begin, apply a generous wash of transfer ink or disperse dye to paper with a large brush or sponge. While the ink or dye is still wet, sprinkle coarse sea salt over the paper. Allow the paper to dry completely. The grains of salt will draw the pigment to them and create gorgeous patterns that cannot be created any other way.

When the dye is completely dry, brush the salt off, and the image will be ready to transfer to fabric. The smallest grains of salt can be difficult to remove, but this won't affect your print adversely. Take care to get rid of the larger pieces of salt, however, because they are very gritty, will prevent smooth ironing, and may even tear the paper.

This is one process where transfer products are not interchangeable. Thicker transfer paints really don't work well with salt unless you dilute them a little bit with water; even then the results are less dramatic.

As you can see in the bottom photo at right, salt-textured papers can resemble lichen. In a different color—depending on your imagination—they might be a night sky of twinkling stars.

The salt technique is one of my favorites for creating backgrounds, and it is so easy to get beautiful results every time. Simple shapes are more interesting because of the visual texture of the color. Salt papers were used as backgrounds and motifs in the samples shown at right.

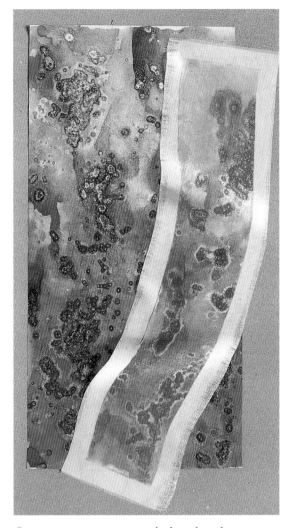

Create gorgeous patterns with the salt technique.

Use you imagination to describe these salt-textured papers

Positive and negative cut shapes from salt-textured paper

Make four-patch unit (shown in quilt above) with salt-textured papers.

SPONGING

A sponge can be used effectively to apply color to paper. Natural sea sponges are an interesting tool, with irregular holes that leave lovely marks in paint. Take care not to overload a sponge with color, or the marks the print makes won't be distinct. Sponge prints can be random, to create texture, or regular, to create a pattern. The sponge-print samples shown at bottom right are made with shapes cut out of compressed craft sponges.

The sponge technique is very easy to do. You can draw on the firm surface of a craft sponge with a pencil to create a guide for cutting, if necessary. After you cut a shape with a pair of scissors, place the sponge in water and allow it to swell. The holes will become very apparent and print lovely, bubbly marks, which will contribute to the charm of your print.

Sponges, in addition to creating distinct print marks, can also be used to drag broad areas of color across a piece of paper. Sponge brushes, available in a variety of sizes from art supply stores, are great for this. They are black foam-rubber wedges with wooden handles, and they are very inexpensive. Try putting three or four colors of paint in a row on a plate. Your colors will need to be thick or they will not remain separate. Dip the edge of a sponge brush into the paints but don't mix them. Drag the resulting stripes of color across the paper to paint a rainbow.

With the sponge technique, let your imagination go. Remember, however, that after you have used a tool such as a sponge to print color, you must use it only for that purpose. Never try to return it to its original use. You might consider cutting shapes from bathroom or kitchen sponges that have seen better days. They will function just as well as craft or printing sponges, but you may find them a bit more difficult to cut accurately. Try marking the shape you want to cut on the sponge with a waterproof, felt-tip pen. Print sponges sold in art and craft stores are hard and compressed for easy cutting; they only become flexible and pliable after they are immersed in water. Take note that these sponges swell considerably in all directions; adjust the size of the shape accordingly, or it may overwhelm your piece of work.

Many techniques employed by interior decorators can also be considered for the transfer technique, although on a more modest scale. Try rag rolling with a scrap of fabric that has been crumpled into a ball, dipped into transfer paint, and rolled across the paper. Try brush dragging with an old toothbrush, or do some stippling with a stencil brush, working with it until it is quite dry to make spiky, thin lines.

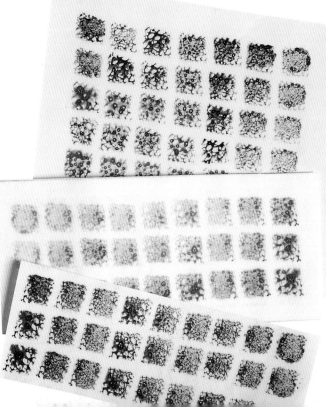

Sponge-print samples made with compressed craft sponges.

SPRAYING

You can put dye solution or ink into a spray bottle and mist it onto paper for a soft, gentle print. Little cosmetic spray bottles or pump-action silk-painting bottles are probably the simplest to use. In theory, plant-misting bottles would also be suitable, but they hold large quantities of liquid and are not good for small projects.

When you're ready to try the spray technique, use an upturned cardboard carton, which can serve as a spray booth and help keep fine mists of color under control. Attach the paper you want to spray to the inner back surface of the box with dressmaking pins or a loop of sticky tape on the reverse. Spray the whole sheet of paper with a single color or use a combination of colors for a random, textured effect that suggests granite or another type of stone.

For a more formal design, mask an area of your paper or make patterns by spraying through an old bit of lace. Create interesting stencils with items you have, such as chicken wire, net bags, paper doilies, or mesh packaging.

If the items you use for stenciling are made of paper, they will earn their keep twice—once as a stencil and then again flipped over for transferring an image.

Stone effects with the spray technique

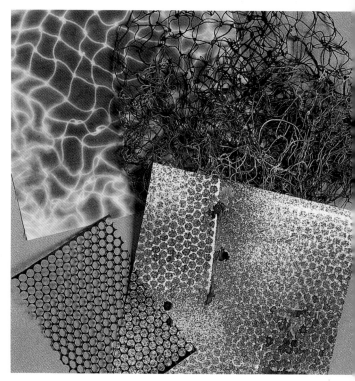

Interesting stencil effects are possible by using items you have on hand.

Paper doilies work great for masking and transferring an image.

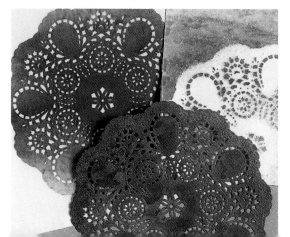

Another spray idea involves taking strips of low-tack masking tape, twisting them along their length as though you were making Christmas garlands, and then sticking them to your paper at the top and bottom. Spray over the tape and remove it when the paper is dry to create a draped fabric effect, as shown in the photo at right.

Inks and powder disperse dyes in solution are suitable for use with an airbrush. An airbrush uses compressed air to force a very small amount of paint to cover a large area. It produces a very fine mist of color, less grainy than with a pump spray. You can exercise great control over the gradation of color and tone with an airbrush. Notice how gently the feather shades across from yellow to soft green in the photo below.

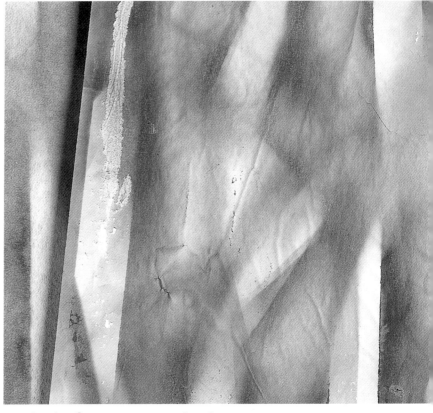

Results of spraying over twisted masking tape

Color gradation with an airbrush

Over-spraying with an airbrush produces runs of color, which can add interest to background fabrics.

If you do not flush out the reservoir in your airbrush between changes of color, you will achieve a smooth transition from one color to another. Make sure to mix the dye well, because lumps can block the nozzle of the airbrush. While this is not harmful to the airbrush, it is frustrating to have to stop and clean the needle when you are in the creative mode. Some of the samples shown in the following photos make use of what might be considered faults in proper airbrushing. Overspraying (shown at bottom right of previous page) produces runs of color. I use this effect purposely to add interest to large areas of background fabric. Spraying too long and too close to the paper makes strange "alien flowers" as shown below.

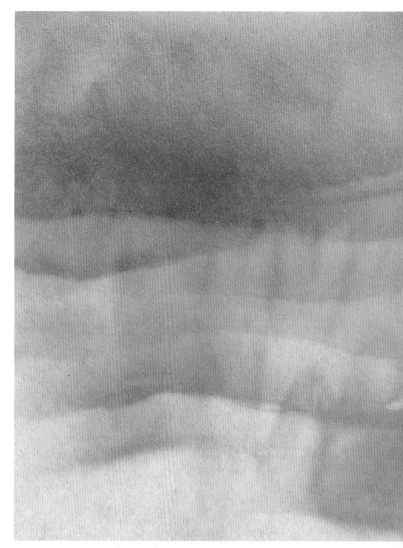

Create a landscape look by spraying across the torn edge of paper.

It is fun to exploit these quirky effects and use them as details on a transfer project. For example, an airbrushed "landscape" made by spraying repeatedly across a torn edge of paper could easily be a candidate for the addition of some foreground plant detail. See the fabric sample above.

Remember, however, the importance of working safely around sprays. The particles of dye are so fine that they float in the atmosphere and constitute a breathing hazard to anyone in the room—not just the artist! Always wear a mask and follow the manufacturers' guidelines for safety.

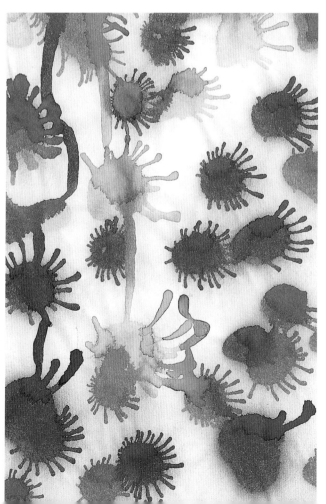

"Alien flowers" made with an airbrush

STENCILS AND MASKS

Commercially produced waxed-paper stencils are an easy solution for printing motifs quickly and easily. The example in the photo below was made by placing a stencil on top of a piece of white poly/cotton blend, putting a sheet of prepared paper—blue transfer-color side down—over the stencil, and ironing the color through the stencil "window." I added strips of scrunch-printed transfer borders (see page 26) and machine quilted the white background areas.

Cut paper shapes are also very simple to use and really effective. I return to this method over and over again because the results are both predictable and pleasing. The prints have lovely, crisp edges. The feather print shown on the facing page, and the strange, square spirals shown in the photo below were made this way.

Results from a commercial stencil

Cut paper in the shape of square spirals and the printed fabric.

Positive and negative prints made with paper feather.

There is an added bonus when working with a paper mask. The mask will take on color from the paper with transfer color and can be flipped over and used for printing.

I drew the feather shown in the photo at left freehand, but if the idea of drawing worries you, read the section "You Can't Draw? So Cheat with a Photocopy!" on page 60, or trace a suitable shape from a book or magazine. If you cut your mask carefully from your sheet of paper and the background remains intact like a frame, you can also print with the frame. Use a small, sharp craft knife or embroidery scissors with pointed blades to help negotiate tricky shapes. Place the mask on the fabric to be printed, and position a sheet of prepared paper, color side down, over the mask and fabric. Press through a sheet of parchment paper until the transfer is complete. Alternatively, you can also cut your mask shape and frame from a sheet of prepared paper and make two separate prints from each.

Spraying also works particularly well with masks and stencils. The grainy quality of dots of color creates an interesting visual texture. It can be very effective to spray one color over another for sensitive and delicate color mixing.

A design that uses both negative and positive shapes twice each and alternates the prints to create a four-patch unit could be used to produce a lovely pillow front or larger item.

To gain more control over really complicated shapes, try using freezer paper instead of plain paper to make your masks. Draw or trace a design on the matte side of a sheet of freezer paper and carefully cut it out. Iron the waxy side of the freezer paper cutout to a sheet of photocopy paper. The heat of the iron will secure the design and hold it in place while you spray your inks or dyes. The close contact of the freezer paper to the photocopy paper helps prevent color from bleeding under the edge of the mask, but take care not to wet it too much or the freezer paper will lift up. If you spray too much color, the color will run on the paper and you will have streaks. (This is actually quite attractive and not really a problem if you think of it as a special design effect!) When the paper is completely dry, peel the layers apart. You will have two printing sheets

for the price of one—a positive shape and the negative sprayed background.

The freezer paper shapes have a tendency to curl after they have been removed from the photocopy-paper background, but they will flatten out again when you print with them. They will also attach themselves to the underside of the parchment paper as you iron and print, which helps keep them flat and ready for the next print. Sprayed papers can be used as single motifs, or positive and negative shapes can be combined for a different look.

Another type of stencil or mask can be made with paper doilies that are sprayed with transfer dye in a pump-action bottle. Lacy paper doilies avoid the time-consuming effort of cutting out shapes. In the example below, the subtle colors were the result of using up the remains of a mixing palette at the end of a

Cut complicated mask shapes from freezer paper, and iron to photocopy paper for successful results.

Additional examples of paper doilies used as masks and for transfer printing

painting session. Doilies could also be cut into quarters and used to print a "cheater version" of the quilt block pattern Drunkard's Path.

Transfer crayons can also be used over a freezer-paper shape that has been ironed to plain paper. Scribble wildly to make lively marks; then peel the papers apart as before. The edge of the mask will give a nice crisp line that contrasts well with the scribbled colored marks.

For added texture, scribble over the paper while working on a textured or relief surface. Any surfaces used for rubbings will work as long as you choose a strong but lightweight sheet of paper.

As described on page 39, torn edges of paper make an effective mask and when repositioned and sprayed over several times, can suggest a landscape or ripples on water. Try using torn strips of freezer paper ironed in place temporarily. The strips will peel away quite easily, and once again the color that transfers to the mask will produce a print if the mask is turned over and ironed to fabric. This technique would work well with transfer crayons too, but avoid using just the points of the crayons. Positioning the crayons flat to the paper will release more color and make more definite marks. Dragging the crayon color off the edge of the mask shape will create a halo around a voided or empty area, as shown below left.

The opposite of the halo effect is achieved by taking the color into a window opening, as shown below right.

 Warm crayons release their color more readily than cold ones and will drag less on paper.

Drag crayon off the edge of the mask shape.

Take crayon color into window opening.

DISCHARGE PRINTING

You can make papers with transfer color more interesting by printing on them with household bleach, which removes areas of color. This technique is known as discharge printing and is most effective when worked on dry, painted paper. Leave the bleach print to dry and then transfer the design in the usual way.

Discharge printing works with dyes and inks, but it is not very successful with thicker paints. Good-quality bleach is fine straight from the bottle. Treat it with the respect it merits and you should not have any problems. As you would expect, dark dye colors are most effective with this technique because there is a greater contrast between them and the bleached print shape. Never use bleach with good paintbrushes, because it destroys the brush bristles. Instead, try printing with wooden blocks, sponge shapes, lino blocks, eraser stamps, and found items such as bottle tops and thread spools. Whatever you use will probably only survive for a limited time, so make sure it is something you consider expendable. If you make a mistake by getting bleach on a spot where it wasn't meant to go, you can easily add more transfer color to repair the damage. (Wait until the bleach is dry, however, before adding more dye, or the bleach will eat into the new color.) Always work on dry paper, or the bleach will spread wildly out of control. As always, let the paper dry before printing from it. There is something magical about discharge prints, which have a luminous quality that cannot be achieved in any other way.

The example shown on page 45, bottom left, is a combination of simple shapes on a cream polyester-and-wool blend (65 percent polyester and 35 percent wool). This might

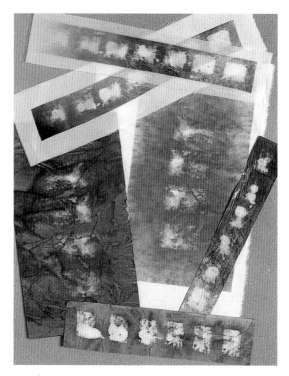

Discharge printing uses household bleach to achieve luminous results.

seem like an unusual fabric for quilting, but it has a lovely surface and shows quilting stitches very well.

This fabric would be a good choice for wearables, too, as it is soft and fluid and doesn't crease. The Nine Patch block center motif was made with a square of paper, which was painted with turquoise transfer dye. A sponge dipped in thick bleach was used for the discharge printing. The paper was allowed to dry, and then the image was transferred to the fabric with an iron. Individual cut-paper shapes, positioned and transferred, were used to create the column of squares. The effect was too stark for my liking, so I placed a large sheet of paper with yellow transfer color over the whole fabric area and transferred the color to tone down the intense blue and add some background color to the cream base. After adding hand-dyed cotton border strips to the top, bottom, and sides, I layered the piece with polyfelt batting and backing and used free-motion machine stitching to define the contours of the printed areas. Free-motion machine stitching allows the fabric to move freely under the foot of the sewing machine. Because the feed dogs are lowered, the stitch length is determined by the speed at which you run the machine and feed the fabric under the foot. A good reference book for this technique is *Machine Quilting Made Easy!* by Maurine Noble (That Patchwork Place, 1994). By quilting the background densely, the printed shapes, by contrast, have a greater relief. Three colors of embroidery thread were used to add interest and texture.

To demonstrate how different the same print can look with another treatment, take a look at a second example, shown below right. It began with exactly the same piece of paper with turquoise transfer color from the project at bottom left, printed to the center of a silky polyester fabric. Yellow cut-paper squares were added as a second print, and finally the whole fabric piece was printed with a pink-red layer. It has been hand quilted densely by my daughter, Laura, with commercial space-dyed embroidery threads. Laura introduced the colors of the transfer print into the border fabric by working with pink and yellow threads, an effective way of creating a harmonious piece.

TIP Transfer products work on synthetic threads as well as fabrics. Try machine embroidering with polyester threads onto a cotton fabric; then apply color from a sheet of paper with your transfer design. The synthetic threads will pick up the color in an intense way and will contrast beautifully with the fabric background.

Discharge-printing design transferred to cream polyester-and-wool blend, with hand-dyed cotton border strips and machine quilting

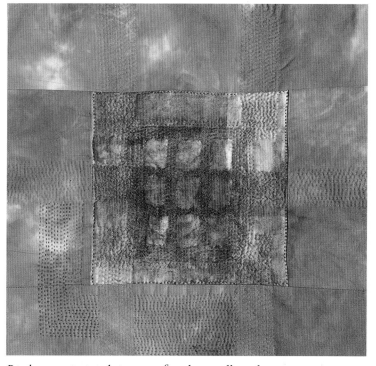

Discharge-printing design transferred to a silky polyester fabric and hand quilted

MONOPRINTING

Transfer paints straight from the jar, or inks and dyes thickened with their appropriate product, are great for monoprinting.

To make a monoprint, take a sheet of acetate or plate glass with smooth edges (tape them down for safety) and apply a thin layer of color with a brayer, which is a type of roller. Be stingy with the color you use; if you are too generous, the paint will be difficult to control and color will flood back into the lines or channels you draw in the wet surface with a pencil eraser or something similar. Draw quickly, because the color will soon dry and become unworkable. The channels you make in the paint should be fairly distinctive. Once you are happy with your drawing, place a sheet of paper onto the surface and apply gentle pressure to make a contact print. You can use a roller to do this or just your hands. (This technique requires a careful approach. The pressure you apply to the paper can obliterate finely

Monoprints on paper and fabric

Try overprinting with your monoprint (printing over earlier prints).

drawn lines by squeezing the color into them.) Peel the paper off the glass or acetate, and put it aside to dry.

It is unlikely that you will be able to make a second print, which is why this technique is called monoprinting. But if you decide to try, you'll probably need to add more paint. When the monoprint is dry, transfer the image to pale fabric or fabric that is already colored by an earlier print.

Overprinting might be a good way of redeeming a weak piece, or subduing one that is too bright. For a design to stand out clearly, try working with a darker paint if you use your monoprint for overprinting.

Monoprints with black, scratchy lines look good when transferred to a plastic-wrap, textured background print of medium to light value. Try a variety of implements to make marks in the paint. Use a plastic hair comb, or cut sharp grooves into a strip of cardboard. The plastic grooved comb normally used to apply tiling adhesive also makes lovely marks. The samples below left show scratchy marks made with the wrong end of a paintbrush.

If you want to sign your work or have lettering in your design, monoprinting is a great technique to use. The process of printing first to paper and then to cloth reverses and then reverts the direction of the letters. What you see on the glass plate is what you will get on your fabric. You can also try replacing the glass with aluminum foil, plastic wrap, or a plastic bag for rolling out your paint. Create a few creases for texture before rolling or painting on the layer of paint. Aluminum foil is especially good at holding sharp creases, but all of these things are delicate materials that will tear if gouged with sharp tools, so be careful when drawing your lines. This monoprint process is also quite effective for creating linear, textural marks on the paper without using any drawing at all. Monoprints are quick, so do several at a time to make better use of your time. For variety, try adding a different color to the acetate or foil after each print. The vestiges of color left behind will slightly affect subsequent prints. Finally, before you begin to clean up your tools and equipment following a monoprinting session, roll your brayer across some clean, white paper. It is surprising how often this produces interesting colors and marks that print beautifully. Think about other ways you can be inventive with monoprints!

Use the wrong end of a paintbrush to create scratchy marks in monoprints.

STAMPING

Stamps made from a range of materials work very well with transfer paints. Thicken the inks or dyes you use with the appropriate product, and they, too, will be equally successful with this technique.

I like to make my own stamps from plastic erasers. I can cut them quite easily with a lino-cutting knife and include as much fine detail as I want. I can also line them up for repeat designs and change the direction of the print or stamp to build an interesting pattern. Another type of stamp, made from foam rubber, is available at most craft stores and toy shops. Foam-rubber stamps are simple to use, and they achieve excellent results. I like the texture created when you lift a foam stamp away from the paint on the paper.

Press and lift stamps away from paper.

TIP Many stamped samples are transfer printed onto sheer fabrics, and it is fun layering them over an opaque fabric print to make a more complex design. The color intensifies when transparent prints overlap each other. Shadow appliqué or layered designs would be effective worked this way, defining each shape with space-dyed embroidery thread.

RUBBINGS AND RESISTS

Resist techniques are fun to try, and they offer a way of combining transfer crayons with paint or ink. Resist techniques rely on the fact that oil and water do not mix—or wax and dye, or any product that seals parts of a surface and prevents a water-based ink, dye, or paint from reaching that surface. To begin, take a transfer crayon and peel away the protective paper so that you can use the whole length of the crayon, not just the point. Put a sheet of paper over your chosen print block or item to rub over, and hold both firmly. It is important that nothing moves while you are working, or you will get a blurred image. Make a rubbing by gently passing the crayon back and forth across the surface until the desired amount of detail has been captured. You can make rubbings from items such as a design made with string affixed with craft glue to a piece of cardboard, a lino cut that you have previously made, or a commercially produced wooden printing block.

Transfer crayon rubbing printed to fabric

Transfer printing results with lino block

Transfer crayon rubbing and transfer paint or ink wash on paper

Fabric printed with transfer crayon rubbing and paint or ink wash

You can also track down interesting surface textures around your house and garden. Try fence posts, concrete paths, ceramic tiles, textured wallpapers, metal grids, and waxy leaves with well-defined veins (the undersides of leaves usually provide better definition than the tops). Some of the examples here were made from a plastic construction game for children.

Rubbings are so quick and so economical that it is a good idea just to experiment and see what is most pleasing to you. The paper you use for this technique needs to be strong enough to take the pressure of the transfer crayon yet fine enough to show the detail of the texture being rubbed onto it. Be selective, and choose textured images that you like. When doing rubbings, it is almost impossible not to create an untidy outer contour where the crayon has slipped off the edge of the item below, so take a pair of scissors or a craft knife and cut a clean edge around the design if you like. Paint a wash of transfer ink over your finished rubbing. The waxy crayon will resist the watery ink. This technique also works with transfer paint, but it helps to dilute the paint a little with water to assist the resist. Allow the paper to dry completely before printing. You will find that the crayon transfers faster than the ink, so keep pressing until both mediums are visible on the fabric.

With resist, your color and value choices are really important. If you choose the wrong combinations, there will not be enough definition to show your designs clearly. Try using black crayon with a bright color ink, or complementary colors. Try using several colors in a rubbing for a more sophisticated result. Test how each color actually transfers to fabric, because they are not

If you are really careful and have a bowl of water standing by in case of accident, it is fun to work with a lighted candle. Allow drops of wax to fall onto the paper; if you hold the paper flat, the drops will form dots; if you tilt the paper the wax will run like raindrops.

always the same as they appear on paper. When you print, the melting wax seems to inhibit further transfer of the colors, so second prints with this technique are both disappointing and rarely worth the effort unless you are aiming to produce a very pale fabric.

Household candles can be used in a similar way as crayons. The resulting print will have voided areas where the base fabric color is preserved by the colorless wax. To do this technique, allow a lighted candle to melt and drip wax onto your paper in a pattern of your choice. Paint as before, with dye or slightly diluted paint. Let the color dry completely. When you are ready to print these inked sheets, remove as much of the wax as possible with a fingernail or small knife. If you don't, it will melt into the fabric and be difficult to wash out (although a really hot wash with detergent should do the trick if necessary). Any of the techniques that involve transfer crayons and/or wax will affect the hand of the fabric, making it more stiff. This effect can be remedied slightly by washing the fabric, but it will still be discernible. If this is a problem, avoid wax technniques.

In addition to wax and crayons, there is a useful product available from art supply shops that is known either as liquid frisket or artists' masking fluid. This rubber solution can be painted, printed, or flicked onto paper and acts as a resist. It ruins good brushes if it gets up into the metal portion, so use an inexpensive paintbrush that you consider disposable. An old toothbrush can also be put to good use here. Dip the brush into the fluid and drag a knife or your thumbnail across the bristles to flick spots onto the paper. Let the solution dry before painting with ink or paint. You can remove the

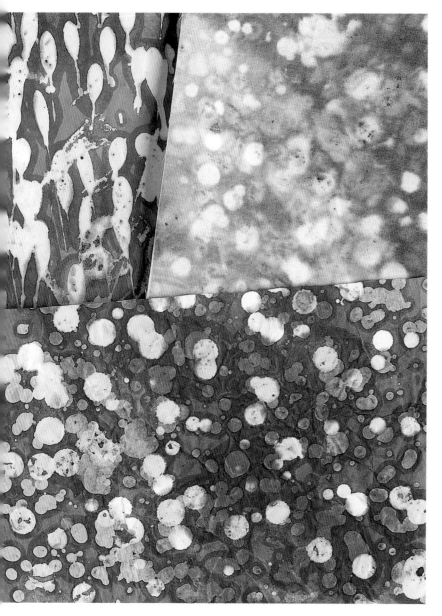

Papers with wax and ink washes

rubbery marks completely or partially by rubbing them with a clean finger, once the color is dry, to reveal the unpainted areas. If a little of the rubber solution remains on the paper, it softens the effect of the print. Try both ways to see which you prefer. The sample below left shows how the rubber solution was painted onto a reversed computer print-out of lettering. The transfer dye was then washed over the dry rubber solution that was only partially removed before printing. Any rubber solution that attaches itself to the fabric can be easily removed by scratching it with a fingernail.

Graphic artists use a product, called artists' frisket, which looks like transparent plastic, comes on a roll, and is self-adhesive. You can cut it easily with a scalpel or craft knife and it can be positioned and repositioned several times. It is ideal for masking areas when using an airbrush because it makes very good contact with the surface. It is a more expen-sive option than freezer paper; however, the expense may be worthwhile because the plastic is strong and durable and will last longer than freezer paper. You can find it at art-supply shops. The feather stencil shown below was made from artists' frisket.

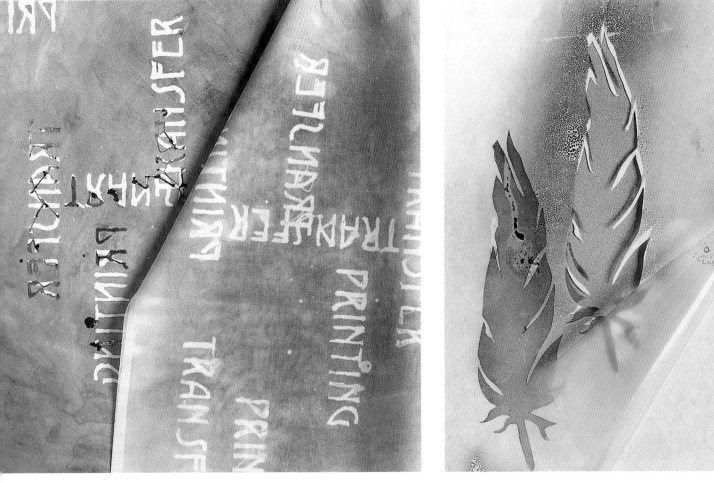

Printed fabric and prepared paper with artists' masking fluid and transfer dyes

Stencil made from artists' frisket

CREATING A
COLLECTION OF PAPERS

Have fun creating lots of papers for transfer printing. Think of them as you would your fabric stash, and vary the colors and textures to provide the same variety you would need for any fabric project. Working with a limited number of colors need not be a problem as long as you keep the idea of contrast in mind. It is pointless to use all the colors you have on each paper, because even if the proportions and designs are varied, inevitably the resulting fabrics would become too similar. Try painting a sheet of paper red, for example, and then a sheet of blue. Mix a little red into the blue for a third sheet, and then add even more red for a fourth. Before long, you will have produced a complete range of colors. This family of papers will work well together because they are related to each other in a very harmonious way.

Use almost exhausted painted papers to print a hint of color on your fabric.

You can also work with the same two colors and vary the texture from sheet to sheet with the techniques described earlier. Imagine how interesting your resulting collection will be. All the design fundamentals relating to any type of textile work apply here, but none of them is more important than the value of the colors you use and the contrast you achieve. Involve some lights, mediums, and darks in the same way you do when creating a patchwork design, and remember that the base fabric can be left unprinted in some areas to provide necessary quiet, pale space. Think of any unpainted paper as an open window that will allow the color of the fabric to show through the rest of the print. Remember, too, that the papers will become paler after a couple of prints. Use this fact to your advantage. Even very pale prints can be useful because they coordinate so perfectly with stronger colors. I have a personal dislike of too much white fabric, so I tend to print the merest hint of color from an almost exhausted painted sheet as a final layer for all of my designs, which helps to harmonize the overall color scheme.

Weaving with Painted Paper

Woven strips of painted papers

Another unique way to transfer an image involves weaving strips of painted paper. Try slicing into a sheet of painted paper with a craft knife or scissors. The cuts you make can be straight or curved. Leave a small length of paper uncut at the top edge of the page to keep everything connected. Now cut a plain white sheet of paper into narrow strips and weave these in and out of the painted paper strips. The white paper will mask off areas of the transfer color, preventing it from transferring to the fabric. You can either print the whole sheet to make an attractive basketweave design, or iron through a cut paper shape like the heart shown below.

TIP Machine quilted lines following the print lines will add definition. Try creating interesting grid designs with variations of this idea.

Iron woven design to fabric through a cut heart shape.

Layering

If you plan to create complex designs with several components, it's best to do this in layers. That way, the design can be built gradually until you reach your desired result. I like the control that successive printing gives. I can easily check on the depth of color and adjust it, if necessary. And overprinting with a piece of paper that has an almost exhausted transfer image is just enough to knock back stark white without losing the clarity of the motif I have printed. The lizard panel shown below illustrates this well; there is no white fabric visible because all the areas have been overprinted, sometimes more than once.

When you are sampling new techniques, it is inevitable that you will have some results that are more pleasing than others. Consider this a challenge to your ingenuity, and try to

Overprinted fabrics

redeem the "failures" by overprinting them with a second layer of color. Surprisingly complex images can often occur with this layering technique. And let's face it: if you didn't like the first print, what have you got to lose? The second print still allows some of the underlying color to show but modifies the effect; it's as if you added a transparent layer of fabric. Remember that transparent color will not obliterate the previous layer of color. For example, a red layer over a blue layer will make the fabric purple, and so on. Graphic or linear marks are best added as a final print. This way the colors remain sharp.

Troubleshooting

For success with the actual printing of your wonderful papers, it is vital to follow a few guidelines.

- Work on a firm surface.
- Unless you want a blurred image, do not allow the paper to move on the fabric while you iron.
- Apply heat with a firm pressing action.
- It is important that the iron reaches a high temperature to assist the transfer of the dye, but keep the iron moving slowly or the soleplate will print as a recognizable shape.
- Ironing through parchment paper aids the movement of the iron and helps it slide across the print without disturbing the painted paper below.
- Try to prevent the electrical cord attached to the iron from pulling against the fabric as you work.

Don't be impatient. Many faint prints are due to insufficient pressing time, but it is difficult to be specific on the length of time needed because there are so many variables. The type of fabric and the thickness of your print paper will both affect the results you get, as will the size of your design. A small print that can be covered completely by a household iron in one action will probably not need to be ironed more than a minute or two. A large design, however, will require more pressing time in order to cover the whole area with equal thoroughness. There is no substitute for experimentation and sampling.

Your iron temperature should be as hot as your fabric will allow or the dye will not transfer with any depth of color. If the results you get are brighter than you expected, try overprinting to subdue the color. Also, bear in mind that when you use the fabric, you may be cutting it into smaller pieces for patchwork. It is amazing how this changes the character and appearance of a piece of fabric. To put this to the test, isolate an area by viewing it through a cardboard window. Often, fabrics that appear too bright or crude in large areas improve when "edited" in this way, and it is a closer representation of how they will actually look in a patchwork piece. You can always select the best bits!

SECTION 3

Taking It Further

Continue to discover new and clever ways to work with transfer printing. You can achieve brilliant results with simple techniques like the ones described in this section.

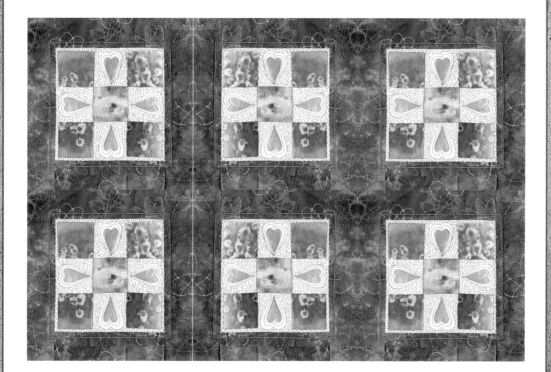

A photocopied dragonfly

Photocopies of a feathers and shells

You Can't Draw? So Cheat with a Photocopy!

Lots of people feel intimidated when asked to draw. There is no doubt that drawing skills are an advantage in many aspects of design, but unfortunately these skills require constant practice and not everyone has the time that this takes. Luckily, we have technology on our side these days, so take advantage of it. The photocopy machine is a wonderful tool, not only for producing copies of things more quickly than we could ever trace them, but also for reducing and enlarging images to the exact size we need for a project.

Newer copy machines can produce mirror images, distort, and tile an image, which opens up all kinds of design possibilities. The simplest application of photocopying for transfer printing is to produce a stencil from a photograph or illustration. Photocopy a picture to the size

you desire, centering the image on the page. Cut the shape from the paper with a craft knife and leave the surrounding frame intact. You now have both the positive motif shape to use as a mask and the negative background shape to use as a stencil. You can create a print with a voided shape and a colored frame by putting the mask onto the fabric, placing a sheet of paper with transfer paint color side down on top, and ironing in the usual way. Using the stencil portion of your photocopied paper will give you a colored motif on a white background. It is also possible to photocopy real objects. The most successful results come from using reasonably flat items, such as scallop shells, feathers, and leaves.

Please note that the photocopy process distorts three-dimensional objects. The farther away from the glass base the object gets, the more the object appears blurred, which may be a problem. However, a dead dragonfly I found did make a beautiful copy. He was very fragile and I had to be careful while photocopying him.

Not only can you use a photocopy to create an accurate stencil, but you can also apply transfer products directly onto a photocopy and take advantage of the printed lines to guide your brush, crayon, or pen. Remember, however, that the image will be reversed during the printing process. This may not matter if the design is symmetrical or an abstract shape. If there is text involved, there are ways you can overcome the problem. Check to see if the photocopier you are using has the capability to print an image in reverse. If so, this is the quickest solution. If not, place the photocopy upside down on a lightbox and trace your design through to the back of the paper. Paint the reversed side and print from that. When ironed, the image will read correctly again.

 **TIP** Work with your own photographs to avoid potential problems with copyright laws, or use copyright-free materials that are available for designers.

Natural Materials as Masks

Using natural objects such as leaves and flowers as masks results in sensitive prints that are very true to the character of the original. Leaves take on color just like a paper cutout, and they can be used to print from as well. Using a combination of both the leaf as a mask and as a print block will give positive and negative shapes.

A leaf cluster was used as a mask in this sample.

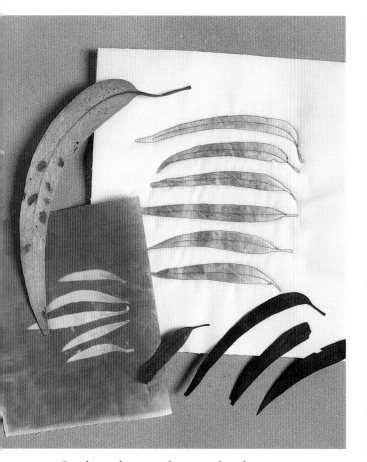

Eucalyptus leaves used as a mask and as a print block

Experiment with a variety of interesting background textures

Dried plant material gives good results and shouldn't stain your fabric. If you are impatient to try fresh leaves and petals straight from the garden, first iron them onto some absorbent paper to blot off any excess moisture. This is a very simple step that will help prevent unwanted sap stains on your finished print. Leaves will be good for several pressings, but they eventually become brittle because of the repeated application of heat. Petals and leaves can be arranged in patterns to make quite elaborate rosettes and garlands, or arranged in precise rows for a completely different effect. I like to place natural objects directly on the fabric and iron a sheet of painted paper over them. That way, I can texture the background color with things like salt, plastic wrap, or brush marks.

There is another method for transferring leaf images. Brush paint directly onto a leaf, allow it to dry, and then print. The leaf shape will transfer accurately, but I think the visual texture of the background that results in the finished print is less interesting than when the leaf is used as a mask. Try both ways—mask and print block—and make comparisons for yourself. Some of the samples here show elegant, slender eucalyptus leaves used first as a mask and then flipped over to make a print.

Before you begin transferring these images, however, consider the scale and shape of the leaves or other natural materials you select for a project. Do they have interesting edges? How, for example, will the leaf shapes relate to the size, shape, and proportion of the whole piece? Maybe real leaves could be combined with cut

Using a real leaf as a mask, and a square of painted paper to create a frame of color on point

Thick vein of feather hinders contact

paper shapes for stems and tendrils. The printed leaf shapes could have detail added, perhaps with stitched veins and stems. The sample shown top left uses a real leaf as a mask over a poly/cotton blend, which has been space dyed in a plastic tray. A square of painted paper textured with salt was placed between the leaf and the parchment paper before ironing to form a frame of color on point.

Feathers employed as masks also make good prints, but if the feather is too thick, the central vein can hinder the contact needed between the iron and the fabric as shown in the photo at bottom left. To solve this problem, consider tracing around a feather to make a paper mask with the same character and detail as the original, or just look for fine, flat feathers. It sometimes helps to ruffle the feather slightly to break up the solid shape and introduce a curved contour for more interest.

Once an image is printed, try following the lines of the print with free-motion machine quilting to create a lovely, fluid design. The small quilt below features detail quilting that follows the lines of a feather shape made with a paper mask.

Detail quilting follows the lines of the feather shape

Create Patchwork Designs with Geometric Shapes

Prepared papers can be cut into simple shapes and used to make faux patchwork designs like the simple Flying Geese border shown below. Once quilted in the ditch, they are quite convincing as patchwork. The triangles can be placed to fly away effortlessly in a curved path, and it beats piecing! Try finding design ideas in any book of quilt blocks. You can tackle really intricate designs, but to gain the control needed to keep the shapes in place, I suggest that you fix the shapes to a sheet of paper to make a print block. The little nine-patch unit shown at right was cut from a sheet of painted paper that had the design drawn on the back. I then glued the cut shapes in place on a corresponding grid drawn on another sheet of paper. Where the white paper became the light areas of the design, I was left with extra shapes of painted paper. I glued these extra shapes to another grid—two blocks in one, and no

Place painted cut shapes on nine-patch grid to create blocks.

wasted paper shapes! The prints that resulted from these print blocks, though simple, work beautifully together, were used several times, and were well worth the few minutes it took to prepare them.

Obviously, the smaller the pieces and the greater the number you have to work with, the more important it is to secure the shapes to a sheet of plain paper. The sample shown at top on facing page combines a Nine Patch block with "appliquéd" hearts .

I colored these papers with dye and textured them with coarse salt. I cut the five squares carefully to size, aligned them, and then glued them onto plain paper with a dab of glue. I cut the four little hearts along the foldline from paper of a contrasting color, and

Flying Geese border

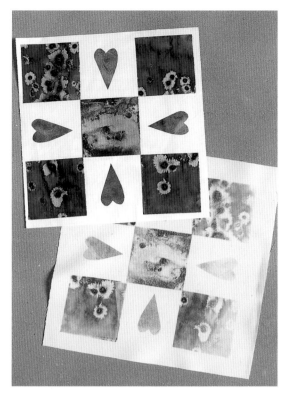

Nine Patch blocks with "appliquéd" hearts

then I glued them in place to complete the design. I printed this "block" to a poly/cotton blend, leaving a margin all around as a seam allowance. I added cotton batik strips as borders on all sides, and layered the piece with batting and backing before machine quilting it with a closely spaced, vermicelli stipple stitch to add texture and flatten the white areas. Notice how the hearts are outlined, or echoed, three times for definition (see photo below).

The areas that are not stitched in this project are effectively raised from the surface because of the surrounding quilting. The same print block can be used several times, but it will become paler each time. For a large project with more than four block repeats, you would need to make additional print blocks.

Detail of quilting on Nine Patch block

SECTION 4

Transfer-Printing Projects

Now that you are familiar with the transfer-printing techniques explained in the previous sections and have experimented to see which ones are your favorites, you're ready to make any of the projects in this section. Bring your own creativity to these transfer-printing projects, and continue experimenting to create new effects with future projects.

Miniature "Patchwork" Quilt

MINIATURE "PATCHWORK" QUILT by Linda Kemshall, 2000, South Staffordshire, England, 6¼" x 8".

With transfer-printing techniques, you can create tiny patchwork designs that would be completely impossible with conventional piecing methods—even foundation piecing. These methods are also useful for making dollhouse quilts.

Fabrics and Supplies

42"wide fabric
8" x 10" piece poly/cotton blend
Graph paper
Black fine-point permanent marking pen
Acrylic ruler
Transfer paint or dye in blue and pink-red
Medium-size artist's paintbrush
Paper-cutting scissors or craft knife
Gluestick
Parchment paper
Rotary cutter and mat
8" x 10" piece cotton or poly/cotton blend
    for backing
8" x 10" piece lightweight polyester batting
Thread for basting
Thread for machine quilting
Tiny beads for embellishment
Embroidery thread for edge detail

Making the Print

1. Draw the design shown in the photo at right accurately on graph paper with a black marking pen and ruler.

2. Make 3 photocopies of the drawn design. Because it would be very difficult to color tiny individual shapes accurately, paint the entire back of one photocopy paper with blue transfer paint and the back of a second one with a pink-red paint. Leave the third photocopy unpainted.

3. When the papers are dry, cut out some of the squares and triangles along the photocopied lines. Using the unpainted photocopy as a base, arrange the colored shapes on it, considering carefully where you want to place the lights, mediums, and darks in the design. Remember that the lightest values can be unprinted fabric, which is achieved by leaving some shapes of the design blank.

Project design drawn on graph paper, and color version of design assembled with painted papers

TIP You will have many more painted shapes than the design requires. Use these to create another quilt arrangement—or two, or three, or four! You will need to make more photocopies of the master design for bases on which to glue these extra shapes.

4. When you are happy with your placement of the shapes, glue all the little pieces in place with a gluestick. I use this form of glue because it doesn't distort the paper, and it dries almost immediately. This is the painstaking part of the operation, but after it is finished you will be able to make several controlled prints very quickly.

5. Referring to the basic printing instructions in "Section 1: Transfer-Printing Supplies and Instructions" on page 8, center the painted "quilt paper" facedown on the 8" x 10" piece of poly/cotton blend. Iron through parchment paper to transfer the color and make the print.

Making the Quilt

1. Place the 8" x 10" piece of backing fabric wrong side up on a flat surface. Add the 8" x 10" piece of batting, and finally, place the printed fabric right side up on top of the batting. Because this is such a small quilt, you will only need to thread-baste at the edges. Working in miniature makes hand quilting somewhat difficult; even the most proficient quilter might have problems making stitches tiny enough to match the scale of the design. I quilted my quilt by machine with a fine white thread, a

darning foot, and the feed dogs down. The hearts in the border were added to match the pretty coloring of the quilt.

2. Using a rotary cutter and acrylic ruler, trim the quilted piece to 6½" x 8".

3. Because regular binding can overwhelm the scale of a miniature quilt, a more effective finishing method is to suggest a narrow binding with a blanket stitch. I added some little beads to embellish the edges of my quilt. To do this, thread a bead onto the needle and attach it to the edge when you do each of the blanket-stitches.

   You can decide whether you want to add a bead with every stitch, or only in selected areas as I did. Refer to the instructions and illustration on page 87.

Close-up of edges embellished with blanket stitch and beads.

Make a second miniature quilt with a simple checkerboard center and a Flying Geese border.

TIP

If you think your quilting stitches look too prominent on such a small quilt, try using invisible thread on the top of your sewing machine. Invisible thread is a colorless, nylon monofilament thread for use on pale fabrics. A smoke-colored nylon monofilament thread for use on darker fabrics is also available. Both are almost invisible.

Garland "Appliqué" Pillows

Hand quilted

GARLAND "APPLIQUÉ" PILLOWS by Linda Kemshall, 2000, South Staffordshire, England, 12" x 12".

These pillows were inspired by Baltimore Appliqué block designs. I am very fond of the look of these old designs, but I lack the necessary patience to work one using usual hand-appliqué methods, so I cheated! While both pillows are printed from the same print design, I made one with white fabric and quilted it by hand. For the other I chose cream-colored fabric and machine quilting. The instructions that follow are for the hand-quilted version, but you can easily adapt them to machine quilting.

Fabrics and Supplies

(for Hand-Quilted Pillow)

42"-wide fabric

15" square poly/cotton blend

Copy paper

Transfer paint in red, yellow, blue, and black

Paintbrush

Paper cutting scissors or craft knife

Plain white paper (large enough for complete design)

Gluestick

Masking tape

Parchment paper

15" square cotton or poly/cotton blend for backing

15" square batting

Thread for machine sewing

Thread for hand quilting

Thread or safety pins for basting

Rotary cutter, ruler, and mat

12" pillow form

Machine quilted

Making the Print

1. Paint one sheet of copy paper with mixtures of yellow and blue paint to make various green leaf colors, and paint another piece with mixtures of red and yellow to produce orange, yellow, and red fruit colors. I recommend that you introduce some visual texture by adding brush marks to the papers for the leaves and berries. Things in nature are rarely flat in color—tonal variations, subtle shadings, and various patterns usually create visual interest and dimension.

 Use a thicker consistency of paint for this print. If you have only dye or ink, thicken it with the product recommended by the manufacturer.

2. I made the stem of the garland design by drawing around a 6" china tea plate onto a sheet of copy paper, but you can also use a compass. Add a second line inside the first to give the stem some width. You can do this by eye. Then turn the paper over and roughly paint the area of the stem shape with black paint. The pencil lines should be visible from the back; if they are not, go over them again and press a little harder until you can see the lines clearly. There is no need to try to keep the paint exclusively within the pencil lines, because you will need to cut out the shape before you print, and that will give it a clean, sharp edge. You also don't need to paint the whole piece of paper, because that would be a waste of paint. You will need to

Use warm colors for fruit and foliage prints.

paint another small area black, however, so that you can cut it up for the short stems.

3. When the paint is dry, fold the paper in half from top to bottom. Refold it in half, from side to side. Press the crease lines firmly between your finger and thumb, and cut out the circular stem shape. Mark horizontal and vertical lines at the center of a large piece of plain paper to establish 4 quarters. Match the drawn lines on the paper to the folded lines on the circular stem to position the stem on the background. Glue the stem in place with just a few dots of glue. Don't be tempted to glue the whole shape down, because you will

need to tuck the individual leaf stems under the edge of the circular stem as you compose the design.

4. Select areas of the colored papers from which to cut out a selection of freehand leaf and fruit shapes. Make the red and yellow fruit shapes slightly more rounded at the ends than the leaves.

If you are uncomfortable cutting leaves without a pattern, draw around an actual leaf on cardboard and then cut it out to make a template.

5. Cut out some narrow strips of black painted paper for individual short stems. I used 15 or 16 stems per pillow. These strips will only need to be about 1" x ⅛". And remember that if your stems differ slightly in size, it will only add to the charm of your finished design.

6. Lay your cut leaves and fruits on the large piece of paper. Place them in a balanced arrangement around your circular stem. The number of shapes you include in your design can vary and depends on the size you cut your circular stem, how close you decide you want to place the leaves and fruits, and the lengths of your individual stems. The lines drawn in step 3 will help you keep a balanced number in each quarter of the design.

7. When you are satisfied with your arrangement, glue the elements of your design down with a gluestick. By using just small dots of glue, you will be able to tuck stems under leaves and the circular stem as the design develops.

8. It will take time to press this relatively large design area. Place the print fabric on a layer of clean white paper, smooth it out, and tape each corner to your work surface with masking tape. Attach more strips of tape along the sides if necessary, to keep the fabric smooth and secure. Referring to the basic printing instructions in "Section 1: Transfer-Printing Supplies and Instructions" on page 8, center the paper with the transfer design facedown on top of the fabric, and tape each corner. Iron through parchment paper to make the print. Try to avoid ironing over the masking tape if you can. These precautions should prevent any problems.

It is all too easy to move the fabric accidentally when working with a large piece, so take care to avoid this as you press.

Paper design glued in place and ready for printing

Making the Pillow

1. Place the backing fabric wrong side up on top of your work surface, and place the batting on top. Add the printed fabric right side up and thread-baste or pin through the layers of the quilt sandwich.

2. The hand quilting I did on my pillow is a simple running stitch worked in a space-dyed embroidery thread for subtle color variation. I particularly like working with this type of thread because it creates the color changes I like without the need to keep rethreading. My stitches are dense. I also kept the tension quite tight and changed the direction of the stitched rows so that the piece did not distort too much. Stitching this densely in a single direction would make a square become rectangular. The unquilted, printed areas are thrown into relief, helping the illusion that they are appliquéd. This type of quilting creates a lovely surface with dimples.

3. Using a rotary cutter and ruler, trim the quilted panel to 13" square. Place it face-down on the fabric that will become the pillow back. Machine sew around the edges with a ½" seam allowance. Leave an opening large enough to insert a 12" pillow form.

4. Turn the pillow right side out, insert the pillow form, and close the seam by hand or machine.

TIP Try "Cheater's Appliqué." From prepared papers, cut out simple shapes that suggest typical motifs used in appliqué quilts. You don't even need to be able to draw for this—you can trace suitable shapes from home furnishing fabrics, wallpaper, rugs, tile, or decorative items in your home. By using a motif already present in a room, you can create a quilt design that will be harmonious with your decor. You can also design panels for pillow covers, tablecloths, table runners, and place mats this way, or trace a shape from a curtain and use it as a border print on sheer polyester fabric to make coordinating window blinds. Folk art is also a rich source of inspiration, with its simple shapes and beautiful colors. Another option is to trace around actual leaves from the garden!

Simple shapes suggest appliqué

Detail of hand quilting

Detail of machine quilting

Fold-and-Cut Wall Hanging

FOLD-AND-CUT WALL HANGING by Laura Kemshall, 2000, South Staffordshire, England, 8" x 8".

Have you ever folded a piece of paper to cut out a snowflake? This intricate motif is cut in the same way. It resembles Hawaiian appliqué designs but it would be almost impossible to stitch with conventional needle-turn appliqué methods, so I cheated and printed it!

Fabrics and Supplies

42"-wide fabric

14" square white poly/cotton blend

Copy paper for painting and trying out designs

Paper-cutting scissors

Transfer paint, ink, or dye in red and green

Parchment paper

14" square cotton or poly/cotton blend for
    backing

14" square batting

Thread or safety pins for basting

Quilting or single-strand embroidery thread
    (flower threads are a good choice)

Rotary cutter, acrylic ruler, and mat

10" square of mount board (available from art-
    supply stores)

Strong thread for lacing over board

White thread for attaching lining

12" square fabric for lining back of mount
    board

Curtain ring for hanging

Making the Fold-and-Cut Print

1. The best way to create the fold-and-cut
    shape is to start by experimenting with a
    few paper-folding exercises. Cut a piece of
    copy paper to exactly 8½" square, fold it
    in half, and fold it again into quarters.
    Then fold it diagonally into eighths, as
    shown below.

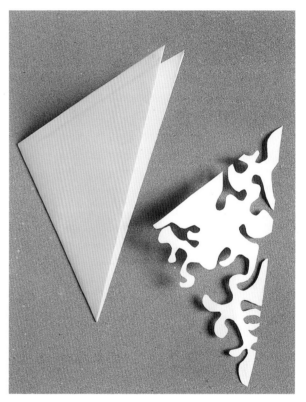

*Paper folded into eighths, before cutting,
and after-cutting results*

2. Using a pencil, draw some curved shapes
    along each of the three sides of the folded
    paper square. Make cuts along your drawn
    lines on both of the folded edges and the
    bottom edge. Make sure to leave some of
    the folded edges intact or the whole thing
    will fall apart when you open it up. Your
    first fold-and-cut designs probably won't

be wonderful; that is why it is good to experiment several times before you start cutting a real design from paper prepared for transfer printing.

3. When you have folded and cut a design you're happy with, fold it back into eighths again. Take a sheet of paper that you have prepared with one of the methods in "Section 1: Transfer-Printing Supplies and Instructions" or "Section 2: Beyond the Basics," and fold it in the same way. For my wall hanging, I painted a piece of paper with a mixture of red and green paint and allowed it to mix and merge on the paper. Place your cut design on top, aligning the folds. Using a pencil, draw around your cut shape. Remove your cut shape and cut out your design from the prepared paper along your drawn lines.

4. Referring to the basic printing instructions in "Section 1: Transfer-Printing Supplies and Instructions" on page 8, print your cut motif. Center the transfer design facedown on the 14" square of a poly/cotton blend. Iron through parchment paper to make the print.

Quilting the Wall Hanging

1. Place the square of backing fabric wrong side up on top of your work surface, and place the square of batting on top. Add the printed fabric right side up and thread-baste or pin through all three layers of the quilt sandwich.

2. Work your first row of quilting stitches along the edges of the print, and add several more rows of stitching to echo the shape. There is no need to mark these quilting lines—just eyeball the distance between rows and maintain about ⅛" of space between them. This may seem like very close spacing, but because the scale of this design is quite small and delicate, wider distances between rows of stitching

Detail of hand quilting; at actual size

would not look as appropriate. Do not quilt right up to the edge of the fabric; leave at least 1" unquilted on all sides. After you finish quilting, the piece will be a little smaller due to the density and tension of the stitches. An allowance for this was made in the original cutting measurements.

Mounting the Finished Design

1. Centering your motif, use a rotary cutter and acrylic ruler to trim the quilted piece to exactly 12" square. Working from the back side, cut the batting and backing fabric another inch smaller on all 4 sides (take great care not to cut into the printed fabric as you do this). This will make the backing and batting the same size as the mount board. Center the mount board on the wrong side of your work, and use strong quilting thread to lace the edges of the print fabric together as shown.

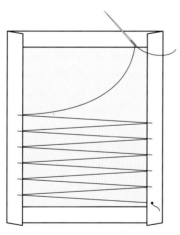

2. Repeat on the remaining 2 sides of the mount board, mitering the corners of the print fabric to minimize bulk, as shown.

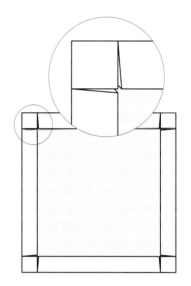

3. Press a fold 1" in from the edge on all 4 sides of the 12" square of lining fabric. Place the pressed lining fabric on the back side of the mount board, and use white thread to stitch it to all 4 edges of the print fabric. For a neat finish, make your stitches as tiny and invisible as possible. Finally, attach the curtain ring at one corner with white quilting thread; oversew (take several stitches in the same place) for added strength. Display your finished wall hanging on point.

TIP Quilt in colors similar to those in your print to coordinate your printed motif with the background and soften the look of the white fabric. My daughter, Laura, hand quilted the "Fold-and-Cut Wall Hanging" by using fine, space-dyed embroidery thread and following the contours of the design.

Creative Variation 1

Exploded design featuring cutouts

Here's an idea for developing this fold-and-cut design further. Incorporate some of the shapes you cut away from your first folded paper. Place the main design at the center of a large piece of paper, and position the cutouts around it to make them appear to explode outward from the center. When you are pleased with your arrangement, glue the pieces in place. This black and white example illustrates this effect.

Creative Variation 2

On-point main motif with layers of tulle

You can also combine leftover pieces to create an on-point main motif. Add triangles to make the design square. I made the red and blue sample shown above by layering 2 squares of orange and 1 square of red nylon tulle over a simple shape cut from freezer paper. I added backing and cotton batting, and free-motion quilted the entire piece to define the shapes. The layers of net intensify the colors and contribute to the richness of the design.

Strip Patchwork Leaf Quilt

STRIP PATCHWORK LEAF QUILT by Linda Kemshall, 2000, South Staffordshire, England, 32" x 45".

This lap quilt contains a selection of transfer prints made by using plant material as masks. A quick foray into my garden produced interesting Hebe leaves and passionflowers, leaves, and tendrils. Gather an array of leaves and flowers in your own garden, looking for pleasing shapes in appropriate sizes. Avoid fleshy or bulky items. Flat shapes with any difficult stalks removed will work best.

Fabrics and Supplies

42"-wide fabric

½ yd. white poly/cotton blend (fiber content of at least 60 percent synthetic) for transfer prints

2¾ yds. assorted light and dark cotton print fabrics for patchwork strips, sashing, and binding

Prepared paper in your color scheme (see "Beyond the Basics," page 24, for ways to create visual texture)

Plant material for masks

Parchment paper

Rotary cutter, acrylic ruler, and mat

Thread for machine sewing

35" x 48" piece of fabric for backing

35" x 48" piece of needlepunched polyester batting

Masking tape

Thread for hand and/or machine quilting

Thread or safety pins for basting

Embroidery thread for blanket stitching

Small beads for embellishment (optional)

Needles (size Betweens) for hand quilting and beading

Cutting

From the white poly/cotton blend, cut:

12 squares, each 6½" x 6½", for transfer prints

From the assorted light and dark cotton print fabrics, cut:

A wide selection of 1½"-wide strips, sorted into lights and darks, for patchwork

4 strips, each 1½" x 45", for vertical sashing

4 strips, each 1½" x 45", for binding

Plant material used as a mask

Making the Prints

1. Referring to "Natural Materials as Masks" on page 61, make 12 prints on the squares of poly/cotton blend. Place plant material such as leaves underneath squares of painted and textured paper. Use the leaves as masks, and create on-point blocks with interesting textured backgrounds. Iron through parchment paper to make the prints.

2. Using a rotary cutter and acrylic ruler, center the print and trim each piece of fabric to exactly 6" square.

Assembling the Quilt Top

1. Sew 1½"-wide strips of cotton print fabric to the top and bottom edges of each 6½" print square, and trim them even with the edges of the block as shown in the illustration on page 86.

2. Referring to the illustration below, sew 1½"-wide strips to both sides of each print square, as in the Courthouse Steps patchwork pattern. I used scraps from my scrap bag and placed lighter colors at the top and bottom of my print squares, and darker ones at the sides.

3. Repeat steps 1 and 2 to add another round of 1½"-wide patchwork strips to each print square.

4. Add 1 more patchwork strip to the top edge *only* of each print square.

5. Add 1 patchwork strip to the lower edge of the 3 print squares which will be positioned at the bottom of your quilt.

6. Sew the blocks together into 3 vertical rows of 4 blocks each. Join these vertical rows together with a 1½" x 45" sashing strip between each row.

7. Add a 1½" x 45" sashing strip to each edge of the quilt to complete the quilt top.

 Make sure you baste the layers at regular intervals to help avoid puckers when you quilt.

Quilting

1. Place the backing fabric wrong side up on a flat surface. It may be helpful to hold edges straight and taut with masking tape. Position the batting on top and smooth out any wrinkles. Add the pieced quilt top with the right side facing up. Working from the center outward, pin or thread-baste the 3 layers of the quilt sandwich together.

2. Quilt by hand or machine as you desire. I used a combination of both techniques, defining each on-point square and the edges of the poly/cotton blocks by hand quilting with a single strand of space-dyed embroidery thread. I also hand quilted the intersections of the border strips so that the crossing lines of stitches suggest a more complex design at the corners of the blocks. I machine quilted the white triangles in the background areas of the poly/cotton squares in white cotton thread. Work a meander-stitch pattern with a darning foot on your machine, and lower the feed dogs. The closeness of this pattern flattens the fabric and draws attention very effectively to the printed motif.

Binding and Embellishing

1. When you finish quilting, use a rotary cutter and acrylic ruler to trim the edges of the quilt straight before attaching the binding.

2. Sew the 1½" x 45" binding strips together to form a strip that is 5 yards long. Fold the binding in half lengthwise with wrong sides together, and press.

3. Starting away from a corner and using a ¼" seam allowance, sew the binding to the right side of the quilt top, mitering the corners as shown below.

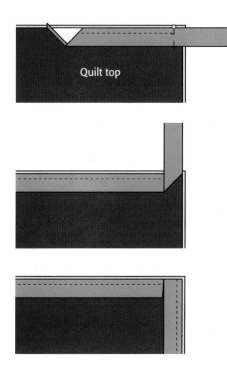

4. Turn the binding over to the back of the quilt, and sew it in place by hand with a whipstitch or blind stitch.

5. I embellish much of my own work with beads. The small, square beads I used here sit very nicely along the edges of a quilt, but round ones are equally attractive. If you want to embellish your quilt with beads, add them with a blanket stitch along the edges of the binding. To do this, thread each bead individually as you make each stitch, and sew the blanket stitches through the binding (bring the needle out at the folded edge of the binding) rather than completely around it as shown below. That way the bead will remain securely at the edge of the quilt rather than rolling around to the back.

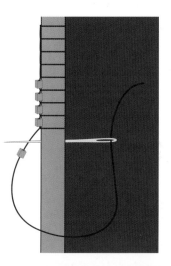

Details of patchwork, quilting, and beaded edge

Lizard Pillow

LIZARD PILLOW by Linda Kemshall, 2000, South Staffordshire, England, 16" x 16".

This fanciful pillow would look great on a garden chair. If lizards are not your favorite animal, you can easily adapt this design to a variety of other creatures.

Fabrics and Supplies

42"-wide fabric

¼ yd. white poly/cotton blend for transfer prints

¼ yd. cotton fabric for sashing

¼ yd. cotton fabric for edge strips

Stencil of a lizard shape cut from paper—retain the lizard shape and the paper you cut it from

Copy paper painted with transfer color. I used dyes in turquoise, scarlet, and yellow, and textured them with plastic wrap. See "Special Effects with Plastic Wrap" on page 33.

Parchment paper

Rotary cutter, acrylic ruler, and mat

Fat-quarter (18" x 22" piece) cotton fabric for quilt backing

18" x 18" square of batting

Thread or safety pins for basting

Fat-quarter (18" x 22" piece) cotton fabric for pillow back

Threads for machine sewing and quilting

16" pillow form

Cutting

From the white poly/cotton blend, cut:

8 rectangles, each 3½" x 6½", for transfer prints

From the fabric for sashing, cut:

10 strips, each 1½" x 6"

1 strip, 1½" x 14½"

From the fabric for edge strips, cut:

2 strips, each 1½" x 14½"

2 strips, each 1½" x 16½"

From the fabric for quilt backing, cut:

One 18" square

From the fabric for pillow back, cut:

One 18" square

Making the Prints

1. Make a stencil and a mask of the lizard shape on page 92. To do this, trace or photocopy the lizard shape onto heavy paper, and use a craft knife to cut the shape out very carefully. Leave the complete positive and negative shapes intact. Do not cut in from the edge of the paper.

Lizard mask and stencil

2. Refer to the basic printing instructions in "Section 1: Transfer-Printing Supplies and Instructions" on page 8. With the 8 rectangles of poly/cotton blend, make a series of prints—some by using the lizard shape as a stencil, others by using it as a mask. The former will produce colored lizards on a white background, and the latter will make white lizards with colored and textured backgrounds. Be sure to iron through parchment paper when transferring images.

No wet color ever goes near masks and stencils with transfer color, so it isn't necessary to use waterproof cardboard for making stencils. Paper is perfectly adequate.

Remember that the masks and stencils will take on color during the transfer process, which means that you can also flip them over and print from them. In addition, you can use them in combination with each other to eliminate all white fabric in a single print. I painted my papers with a mixture of transfer dyes in turquoise and scarlet, and added a touch of yellow to make the greens and oranges. This is where an understanding of color mixing along with the experiments you did in the beginning to determine how various pigments mix together and print, will come in handy. I also used the plastic-wrap texturing technique on page 33 as I painted the papers, to add to the feeling of organic texture.

3. After several prints, your lizard-shaped mask will have taken on some transfer color, so flip it over and make some prints from it. Remember to put a sheet of background color over the top. In this way, you can easily make a colored lizard print with a different color background!

4. Add a delicate layer of color to the white areas. Overprint some of the colors again, leaving the lizard mask in place to maintain definition of shape while allowing more depth of color to be added to the background. When you use both the right and wrong sides of the mask to make prints, you get lizards that face in two different directions. This enhances the dynamic quality of the design and makes it a little more lively. After all, lizards are known for being quick movers!

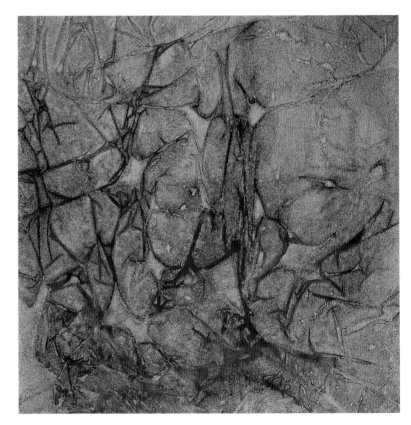

Fabric print textured with plastic wrap

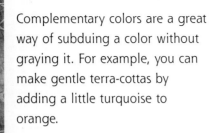

TIP Complementary colors are a great way of subduing a color without graying it. For example, you can make gentle terra-cottas by adding a little turquoise to orange.

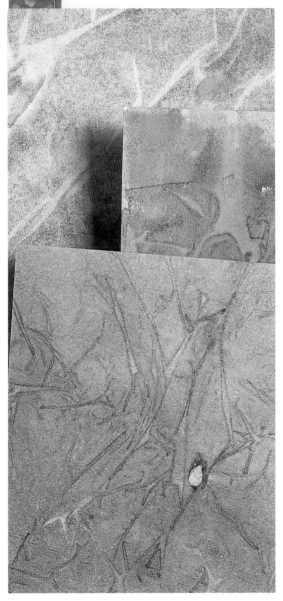

Use pale, painted papers to transfer subtle coloring to the fabric.

Piecing the Pillow

1. Using a rotary cutter and acrylic ruler, trim your lizard prints to 2¾" x 6".
2. Sew 4 lizard print blocks into a horizontal row, with 1½" x 6" sashing strips between them. Repeat to make a second horizontal row of lizard blocks.
3. Join the 2 horizontal rows of lizard print blocks together with a 1½" x 14½" sashing strip between them. Sew two 1½" x 14½" edge strips to the top and bottom edges of the lizard print blocks.
4. Sew 1½" x 14½" edge strips to the sides of the pillow top.
5. Sew the 1½" x 16½" strips to the sides of the pillow top in the same manner.

Quilting

1. Place the square of backing fabric right side down on a flat surface. Place the batting on top, and add the completed pillow top right side up. Thread-baste or pin the layers of the quilt sandwich together; a small piece like this only needs minimal basting or pinning to secure the layers.
2. Machine quilt around each lizard shape and background rectangle. I stitched with the feed dogs down and a darning foot on my sewing machine. This allowed me to stitch in any direction, which is ideal for outlining curved shapes like the lizard.
3. Finish the border by doing 2 rows of machine quilting with the regular presser foot and the feed dogs on your machine raised.

4. Using a rotary cutter and acrylic ruler, trim the edges of the pillow top straight and square. Place the completed pillow top right sides together with the fabric for the pillow back. Stitch around the edges, leaving a large enough opening on one side to insert a 16" pillow form. It is a good idea to overcast the raw edges with a machine zigzag stitch for strength and neatness.

5. Finally, turn the pillowcase right out, insert the pillow form, and close the opening with hand or machine stitches.

 **TIP** By adjusting the print size and maybe the nature of the sashing strips, it would be easy to develop a great design for a quilt.

#

UNITED STATES

Art2Art
PO Box 8370
Springfield, MO 65801
1-800-284-8190
www.Art2Artonline.com
Dritz fabric crayons (transfer crayons)

Dharma Trading Company
PO Box 150916
San Raphael, CA 94915
www.Dharmatrading.com
e-mail: catalog@dharmatrading.com
Deka transfer paints and an extensive catalog

Dick Blick Art Materials
PO Box 1267
Galesburg, IL 61402-1267
1-800-447-8192
www.dickblick.com
Crayola® fabric crayons (transfer crayons)

PRO Chemical & Dye
PO Box 14
Somerset, MA 12726
1-800-2-BUY-DYE
www.prochemical.com
PROsperse disperse dyes and Metaphos thickener

Speed Stitch, Inc.
3113 Broadpoint Dr., Dept. WEB
Punta Gorda, FL 33983-3106
1-800-874-4115
Sulky iron-on transfer pens

UNITED KINGDOM

Art Van Go
16, Hollybush Lane
Datchworth
Hertfordshire SG3 6RE
011-44-1438-814946
Deka transfer paints and an extensive catalogue

BA Marketing (Leicester)
8, Latimer Street
Leicester LE3 0QE
011-44-1162-834202
Fabric design color transfer ink

Fred Aldous
37, Lever Street
Manchester M1 1LW
011-44-161-236-4224
www.safestreet.co.uk/fredaldous
Crayola® fabric crayons and Deka transfer paints

Kemtex Services Ltd.
Chorley Business and
    Technology Center
Euxton Lane
Chorley
Lancashire PR6 6TE
011-44-1257-230220
www.Kemtex.co.uk
Transprint disperse dyes and Indalca PA3R thickener; transfer-printing kits and instructions; advice given on all aspects of textile coloration

Omega Dyes
10, Corsend Road
Hartpury
Gloucester GL19 3BP
011-44-1452-700492
www.omegadyes.fsnet.co.uk
Transfer dyes

Rainbow Silks
27, New Road
Amersham
Bucks HP6 6LD
011-44-1494-862111
www.rainbowsilks.co.uk
Transfer paints, crayons, stamps, and catalog

Vycombe Arts
Fen Way
Fen Walk
Woodbridge
Suffolk IP12 4AS
011-44-1394-380882
Deka transfer paints and an extensive catalog

Whalleys (Bradford) Ltd
Harris Court, Great Horton
Bradford
West Yorkshire BD7 4QE
011-44-1274-576718
Fabrics prepared for dyeing and painting

AUSTRALIA

www.icenet.com.au/-threads
Disperse dyes for transfer printing

About the Author

LINDA KEMSHALL lives in a small country village in South Staffordshire in the heart of England, with her husband of twenty-six years, their two daughters, two cats, and assorted poultry. She works from her studio in a converted pigsty in the garden of their cottage, which dates from 1700, making quilts for exhibition and commission, dyeing and painting fabric, and papermaking. Since 1997, Linda has been the national advisor for patchwork and quilting for the City and Guilds of London Institute, and she also travels widely as an external verifier for the same awarding body. She has taught design and quiltmaking for ten years, in the United Kingdom, mainland Europe, and increasingly, in America. Her quilts continue to be successful in exhibitions in many countries. It is her ambition to extend her teaching and reach many more quilters via the Internet. View Linda's Web site at www.lindakemshall.com.